P9-DKD-805

VOICES OF DEATH

VOICES

OF DEATH

Edwin Shneidman

HARPER & ROW, PUBLISHERS
NEW YORK

Cambridge
Hagerstown
Philadelphia
San Francisco
1817
London
Mexico City
São Paulo
Sydney

Grateful acknowledgment is made for permission to reprint:

Extracts from *Stay of Execution* by Stewart Alsop. Copyright © 1973 by J. B. Lippincott Company. Reprinted by permission of J. B. Lippincott Company and The Bodley Head.

Selections from *The Dwarf* by Pär Lagerkvist, translated from the Swedish by Alexandra Dick. Copyright 1945 by L. B. Fischer Publishing Corp. Renewed Copyright © 1973 by L. B. Fischer Publishing Corp. (now a division of Farrar, Straus & Giroux, Inc.). Reprinted with the permission of Farrar, Straus & Giroux, Inc.

Excerpts from "Notes of a Dying Professor" and "More Notes of a Dying Professor" from a larger work titled *An Autobiography of Dying* by Archie J. Hanlan. Copyright © 1978, 1979 by Mary S. Hanlan. Reprinted by permission of Doubleday & Company, Inc.

Copyright acknowledgments are continued on pages 207–208, which constitute a continuation of this copyright page.

A REGINA RYAN BOOK

For information address Harper & Row, Publishers, Inc., 10 East 53rd Street, New York, N.Y. 10022. Published simultaneously in Canada by Fitzhenry & Whiteside Limited, Toronto.

FIRST EDITION

Designer: Stephanie Winkler

Library of Congress Cataloging in Publication Data

Shneidman, Edwin
Voices of death.
1. Death. I. Title.
BD444.S48 1980 155.9'37 79-2636
ISBN 0-06-014023-2

---

80 81 82 83 10 9 8 7 6 5 4 3 2 1

To my late beloved parents, who only vaguely appreciated that they were the golden sacrificial bridge from a czarist *shtetl* to an American university. Once, after their deaths, when I was in Athens, I sought for their noble prototypes among the voiceless life-size grave reliefs in the ancient Karameikos cemetery, but I learned then that they really lie in my own heart's vault of treasures and that their voices, even in death, speak to me continuously on the beat of my pulses.

Contents

Acknowledgments

In the sense that it took me twelve convoluted months to write this book, the following people provided those kinds of help, assistance and support that *(a)* vastly improved the work from its earlier forms and *(b)* brought it to completion: a peerless editor-agent (with a felicitous combination of golden qualities), Regina Ryan; two helpful editors, Corona Machemer at Harper & Row and Grace Bechtold at Bantam Books; a trio of helper-stenographers: Melinda Bertolet, Jane Neff and Annelisa Frolov; Lois Janis, who graciously made a series of perspicacious editorial suggestions; Donna Stephen, Mary Carol Rudin, Judith Moreno, Deborah Boehm and Carol Heukrodt, who helped me in numerous important ways; Lawrence Pitts, a student in my Death and Suicide course, who gave me the materials from the Auschwitz concentration camps; Eugene Loebl, from whose hands I obtained Vladimir Clementis's letters written in the Soviet prison; Dr. Rollo May, who, in one notable conversation, radically changed the genre of this book; my faculty colleagues at UCLA who read and commented on the manuscript: my valued colleague Miss Nancy Allen, and Drs. Kenneth Colby, Robert Pasnau and Sidney Cohen; and Dr. Louis J. West, chairman of the Department of Psychiatry at UCLA, who permitted me to have a sabbatical leave for a portion of 1978, during part of which Dr. Loma Feigenberg at the Karolinska Hospital in Stockholm was my superb host.

In the sense that I have been working at this book for the past thirty years, three people have given me the stimulation and nurturance without which I would neither have come to any fruition nor have sustained the ideas that made a fruition worthwhile: my beloved mentor, Dr. Henry Murray; my treasured friend, Dr. Evelyn Hooker; and my nonpareil wife, Jeanne Shneidman. And finally, I am deeply beholden to those sterling persons—most now dead—who gave me permission to use their personal documents and, more, gave me the privilege of touching their lives.

Preface

The writing of this book was stimulated by a series of incidents which seemed to happen almost providentially.

In a sense, the book began some thirty years ago—when my interest was first sparked both in the dark side of life (suicide and the dying person) and in personal documents. I stumbled on several hundred suicide notes that had been filed away—their potential value totally unrecognized—in the vaults of the coroner's office in Los Angeles.

Years later, I encountered a young woman at a symposium in a distant state. She told me that she had attempted to burn herself to death. She wanted to tell me about it. I sent her a cassette recorder and tapes. Many months later—the very day after I learned by telephone that she had died—her tapes, describing her life and her immolation, arrived by mail. She asked that her story be told.

Around the same time, a dear professor friend of mine—the late, beloved Dr. Eugene Pumpian-Mindlin—gave me the diary of a thirty-year-old doctor who had died of leukemia. He had kept a remarkably detailed account of the course of his illness and of his reactions to the growing threat to his life. Dr. Mindlin asked me to publish the young doctor's diary in a professional journal which I edited.

Somewhat later, a student in my undergraduate course on death and suicide at UCLA gave me some pamphlets which he had obtained at Oświecim (Auschwitz) during a trip through Eastern Europe. The pamphlets contained documents written by concentration camp victims. The writings had been buried in cans and jars near the gas chambers and had been found in the 1960s.

These sets of materials—each about facing a different kind of death—were devastating for me to read. The stark immediacy of the writing captured my imagination in a way no fiction could. They jogged my memory; I recalled that I had many similar documents that had been given to me over the years by colleagues and patients, and I was driven to look for still other personal accounts of dying.

I believe that these documents contain special revelations of the human mind and that there is much one can learn from them. From that day in the coroner's office, these voices of death have buzzed in my head. This book is an attempt to put them on paper for others to hear.

In the writing I have had several goals: to share with the reader what I know about death and death documents and the theories I have developed about the psychology of suicide, terminal illness and execution; and, at other times, to stand back out of the way so that the reader may have direct contact with the documents themselves; and finally, to show how the different kinds of life-threatening situations are similar to each other and how each is separate to itself.

My hope is that this volume will be only a beginning, a preface to the reader's own subsequent ruminations and self-assessments in his or her journey toward death. In addition, I hope that the book can serve as a guide for readers whose loved ones are dying and cannot postpone the trip. Occasionally, there may be voices that you will recognize from your own experiences, fantasies, dreams or nightmares. When that occurs, then those voices will echo in your mind and you will know intuitively what they are saying.

E.S.

UCLA School of Medicine
August 18, 1979

And lo! towards us coming in a boat
An old man, hoary and with the hair of eld,
Crying "... I come to lead you to the other shore,
To the eternal shades of heat and frost ..."

Dante, *Inferno* (Canto III, "Charon")
Translated by Henry Wadsworth Longfellow

As a historian I had all my life been aware of the extraordinary importance of documents. I had handled hundreds of them: letters, reports, memoranda, sometimes diaries; I had always treated them with respect, and had come in time to have an affection for them. They summed up something that was becoming increasingly important to me, and that was an earthly form of immortality. Historians come and go, but the document remains, and it has the importance of a thing that cannot be changed or gainsaid. Whoever wrote it continues to speak through it. It might be honest and it might be complete: on the other hand it could be thoroughly crooked or omit something of importance. But there it was, and it was all succeeding ages possessed.

Robertson Davies, *World of Wonders*

... I was horribly conscious of something fatally wrong ... I could see no compass before me to steer by; ... Uppermost was the impression that whatever swift, rushing thing I stood on was not so much bound to any haven ahead as rushing from all havens astern. A stark, bewildered feeling, as of death, came over me. ... Look not too long in the face of the fire, O man! Never dream with thy hand on the helm! Turn not thy back to the compass. ...

Herman Melville, *Moby Dick*

1

The Rutters of Death

> . . . with trembling fingers is set down in the log—*shoals, rocks and breakers hereabouts: beware!*
>
> Herman Melville, *Moby Dick* (Chapter 69)

Death is a mystery and we eagerly search for any clues or explanations that we can find. We seek words that will give us solace from our own anxieties and fears. We search for any possible guidelines that will help us avoid the shoals and reefs in the voyages of our own lives.

In the sixteenth and seventeenth centuries—the Age of Discovery—when brave and adventurous Europeans were reaching across the oceans and exploring new lands in America and the Orient, it was vitally important to have whatever guides or maps might be available. Among the navigational logs, there were some special narrative accounts written by pilots who had visited these far-off places. These highly prized guidebooks were called *rutters.* In any potentially dangerous undertaking, it was important to have a pilot who knew something firsthand about the rigors of the journey. A good pilot with a good rutter was as important as a good ship.

A rutter (or routier) was a "Baedeker" made by someone *who had been there before.* It recorded the specific courses between where one was and where one wanted to go; it gave exact soundings; it spoke of the color of water; the nature of the seabed; the pattern of the wind and the currents. A rutter would tell a voyager when to beware of storms and when and where to look for fair winds; it would describe the reefs, the hidden islands, the rocks; but more importantly, it would point out the havens, the safe places, the harbors and the sanctuaries. In a word, a rutter told everything that was necessary for a good voyage. Of course, it did not guarantee a ship's safety, but simply increased the probability of a more calm passage. Above all, it might prevent a disastrous ending.

Just as in the sixteenth and seventeenth centuries navigators used these highly prized guidebooks to avoid the shoals of their own journey, so, I propose, we can now find rutters for our own dying. Death remains mysterious; we scan our horizons for any possible clues that might help us avoid the rough waters in the passage of our lives toward death. Who of us would not want a personal rutter for dying written by a friendly death pilot who had our best interests at heart?

Perhaps the best-known voyage of all time was Ferdinand Magellan's first circumnavigation of the world in the sixteenth century. The journal of that voyage by Francisco Alvo (or Albo or Alvaro), a pilot with Magellan, is an interesting example of an important rutter. Here are extracts from his logbook that relate specifically to the journey around the (now called) Philippines and the Indonesian islands. They were written after the discovery of the straits (later named after Magellan) around the tip of South America, and just before Magellan was killed by natives on the island of Matan (Mactan).

> We departed [in 1521] from Mazaba and went N., making for the island of Seilani. . . . after that we ran N.W., coasting in the island of Bornei until the city itself; and you must know that *it is necessary to go close to land, because there are many shoals,*

> and *it is necessary to go with the sounding lead* in your hand, because it is a very vile coast, and Bornei is a large city, and has a very large bay, and inside it and without it *there are many shoals; it is, therefore, necessary to have a pilot of the country.* So we remained here several days, and began to trade [but] they armed many canoes, 260 in number, and they were coming to take us, and as we saw them we sailed in great haste. . . . [Italics added.][1]

Think of the shoals and the threats to be found in hospital rooms where people are dying of life-threatening illnesses. Sometimes these barriers and shoals take the form of not knowing what to say to a member of the "crew"—a hostile nurse or an overworked intern—not knowing how to deal with certain (emotional) storms, or how to handle certain sudden shiftings of (psychological) ballast or freight in oneself. Voyages on a ship (or stays in a hospital or serious illnesses at home) can be microcosms of larger life where a pilot is almost a necessity, in which it would be helpful to have a rutter like the one of Francisco Alvo.

In the American classic, Herman Melville's *Moby Dick,* there is a chilling interchange between moody Captain Ahab and the mysterious Parsee harpooner, Fedallah. The Parsee gives Ahab a prophetic warning of his own death. What he says is: "Though it come to the last, I shall still go before thee, thy pilot." Later, when Ahab sees the Parsee dead, wrapped in lines around Moby Dick—just before Ahab's own death by the hemp line, exactly as the Parsee had predicted—Ahab shouts to the world: "Aye, Parsee, I see thee again.—Aye, and thou goest before."

Now, obviously I have not "gone before." But at the beginning of this voyage that you and I shall take together, I need to say that I have had some experience as a thanatological—from Thanatos, the Greek god of death—pilot. I have worked for years with both suicidal and dying persons, attempting to dissuade some persons from making their trips and attempting to pilot others, whose trips could not be stayed, in their emotion-fraught passage across the river Styx.

As part of my own work with people dying of serious diseases, I have studied their personal accounts, both spoken and written. For over a quarter of a century I have dealt as well with the psychological turmoil and torture of suicide and suicide attempts; I have examined literally thousands of suicide notes.

It is clear to me that we stand to gain a great deal from a careful perusal of such writings. The "personal documents"—the phrase is from Professor Gordon Allport's pioneer monograph on this subject[2]—of death are, by and large, motivated by the intention to reveal some deep and perhaps hidden aspects of the inner person. The writer often seems to be talking directly to you. Sometimes you can almost feel you are that person (and suffer intensely with that person). And even if you remove yourself somewhat to study the documents, your compassion for that other person can still remain intense. Joyce Carol Oates has put the case precisely when she says that of all forms of literature, the personal document is perhaps the most seductive. "It is the 'easiest' form—the easiest to read and to write; it is authentic, one keeps reading, hypnotized by the conviction *this is real;* therefore it must have value."[3]

Personal documents include any nonfictional autobiographical materials in which the author is being more or less candid about himself or herself, such as personal letters, diaries, journals, logs, confessions, reminiscences, memoirs and autobiographies. Today, of course, technology has brought us another form of personal document: the tape-recorded account—whether recorded by oneself or with a therapist.

According to Allport, the motivations for writing or talking out these personal accounts vary greatly: a desire for order, seeking personal perspective, relief from tension, assisting in psychotherapy, redemption and confession, public service, and the desire for immortality are among the most common motivations. These same motivations apply, of course, to the dying person.

The desire for immortality seems to be one of the strongest drives in those who write about their dying. Marie Bashkirtseff, a well-to-do young Russian woman dying of tuberculosis in nineteenth-century Paris, wrote her now famous diary in secret. But paradoxically (and understandably), she worried about the awful possibility that after she died her family might, finding it, destroy it and then ". . . in a short time, of me there would remain nothing—nothing—nothing! This is the thought that has always terrified me; to live, to be so filled with ambition, to suffer, to weep, to struggle, and, at the end, oblivion! as if I had never existed."

There is a word to describe this circumstance that is even worse than the end of life, worse than naughtment. It is what Melville called being "oblivionated."

Some who write facing death often do so because they want others—after they are dead—to know how it has been, and especially what the tribulations and pitfalls (as well as the occasional triumphs and illuminations) have been. These are very special rutters, written by people who almost self-consciously have attempted to act as death pilots for those who will come after.[4]

Most of us find private and personal documents of death to be fascinating and spellbinding. This may very well be so because there is an element of voyeurism involved: we are allowed to look at thoughts and secrets of the heart that we ordinarily would not be permitted to see. These documents show us the very insides of someone, including the most powerful kinds of human drama, involving (as drama often does) the deep emotions of another human mind that the usual person—unless he is a professional psychotherapist—is never privileged to see.

Personal diaries, journals, letters and notes written by dying persons thus capture our interest in a unique way. We have the strongest yearning to believe that these magical documents will let us in on some special secrets of those aspects of human existence we want to know most about: love, sex, our distant roots, our immediate future and our own death. I believe that if we will listen attentively enough to the voices of the past, some of our yearnings may be fulfilled.

Part One

Self-Destruction

2

Return from Death: Reflections of Fortuitous Survivors

> When both glasses were filled, Charlemont took his, and lifting it, added lowly: "If ever, in days to come, you shall see ruin at hand, and, thinking you understand mankind, tremble for your friendships, and tremble for your pride; and, partly through love for the one and fear for the other, shall resolve to be beforehand with the world, and save it from a sin by prospectively taking that sin to yourself, then will you do as one I now dream of once did, and like him will you suffer; but how fortunate and how grateful should you be, if like him, after all that had happened, you could be a little happy again."
>
> Herman Melville, *The Confidence-Man* (Chapter 34)

In Greek mythology, Charon was the aged boatman of that special skiff that crossed the river Styx from this world to the next. It was clearly to one's advantage to be on good terms with him even though the one-way trip was a relatively short one. He made the return trip by himself, free of human freight. He was the only person in this world who routinely visited the other world and returned. "What's it like?" is a question that nearly everyone then alive would have liked to ask him. But part of his reputation is that he was a morose, grisly and laconic old man, totally uncommunicative about the other side.

In our own contemporary world, there are, however, some people who have planned to make the trip and did everything necessary to leave this world, and then, almost magically, remained in it. These are the rare individuals who have fortuitously survived a suicidal attempt which by its very nature would almost always be a lethal act. I knew an individual who shot himself in the head, the bullet coursing up and under his scalp and coming out the other side, nicking his ear, but not entering the brain case. Extended reflections by such fortuitous survivors can tell us a great deal about what that kind of death scenario is like—the very "inside" of the act of suicide; a near-death (or "return from death") experience.

Retrospective personal reports of near-fatal suicidal incidents are almost mystical documents. They require a narrator (like Melville's Ishmael) who miraculously survives against the greatest of odds in order to tell the tale. Two such cases will be cited in detail in this chapter. The first is that of a young woman who jumped from a high place and was not killed. The second example, also a young woman, is of a tormented person who, while in her small car, poured a gallon of gasoline over her body and then set herself on fire, literally exploding into flames. A few passers-by, with great heroism, pulled her out and rolled her on the wet grass. Several months afterward we met and talked. Some weeks after that, she dictated (especially for me) a lengthy set of reflections, which she completed just a few days before she died of a heart attack.

These admittedly unusual reflections on near-fatal suicide acts provide us with important insights and information, specifically telling us that certain kinds of behaviors are conspicuously poor ways of preparing for a happy voyage through life. The story of these lives—not the details of the suicide—might be called "negative rutters." They are maps that are known to be flawed because they give us misdirections; thus their chief use is as a corrective; they tell us what routes not to take, what turns not to make and what channel markers have been misplaced and are thus dangerously misleading.

"Negative rutters" are lists of things *not* to do; behavior patterns to avoid; types of personal relationships to shun; places (in life) where it is best not to stop or tarry. But these negative rutters also show us what it is like to die and thus may serve the positive function of taking some small portion of the terror and the mystery out of dying itself.

When we look closely at the two suicidal lives that we are going to examine, it is important to bear in mind that all suicidal acts do not have death as their intended goal. Suicidal acts range in their deathful intention or lethality from low (not wishing to die) to high (where death is actively sought). An act of low or medium mortal risk that uses the methods ordinarily associated with suicide (wrist cutting or pill ingestion) may have different psychological components than an act (shooting or jumping) that has obviously fatal intentions. Obviously, *any* suicidal act, whatever its degree of lethality, betokens a genuine psychiatric crisis, and reflects considerable inner psychological disturbance.

A fatal suicide act can be understood—psychologically—as being comparable to a dynamite explosion. Dynamite consists essentially of nitroglycerin, saltpeter and some carbonaceous material such as charcoal; the explosion is sparked by the application of heat. In a somewhat similar way, a deadly suicidal act has three main components and requires one triggering process.

The first element in a serious suicidal act is an unsettled life pattern in which one acts against one's own best interests, reduces one's prospects for happiness, provokes reactions against one's self and, in general, ruins one's own life and career. Examples might include a series of imprudent marriages, excessive use of alcohol or drugs, counterproductive behavior with one's bosses or colleagues at work and generally poor ways of handling problems of physical health, work or interpersonal relations. The best way to describe this pattern is that one behaves as though one were one's own worst enemy. I have named this pattern *inimicality*—a word formed of the Latin root for "friend"—meaning that a person is "unfriendly" not only to others, but to the self.

The second component is increased psychological disturbance in the person's life—what I have called *perturbation.* Being perturbed includes being more than usually anxious, frightened, worried, depressed, agitated. It is synonymous with "being upset." The suicidal person is in a state of heightened disturbance. He or she feels especially boxed in, rejected, harassed, unsuccessful, hopeless or helpless. Perturbation can manifest itself in excessive withdrawal or in heightened activity, and in other patterns of disturbance as well. In general, it is a condition in which the negative emotions (guilt, fear, shame, uncertainty, vulnerability) have the upper hand.

The third ingredient is *constriction:* a narrowing of the range of perception, of opinions and of options that occur to the mind. The person is not only opinionated and prejudiced, but more importantly, suffers from a kind of "tunnel vision." One's ordinary thoughts and loves and responsibilities are suddenly unavailable to the conscious mind. It is not that a person simply "forgets" that, for example, he or she is married; it is far worse —the ties to the spouse are suddenly blocked out and they disappear. The suicidal person turns his back on his own past and permits his memories to become unreal; thus they cannot serve to save him. In this state of tunnel vision and narrowed outlook, the mind is focused almost entirely on the unbearable emotion and, especially, on one specific (and arbitrarily selected) way to escape from it.

An important characteristic of constriction is a tendency to "either/or" thinking. The world is divided into two (and only two) parts—good *or* bad, love *or* hate, a desired life *or* a "necessary" death. Such dichotomous thinking in the suicidal person is characterized by words like "always," "never," "forever," "either/or," and especially the word "only." When the mind constricts, the anguished person sees only the mechanism for stopping the anguish—and that leads us to the triggering process.

Just as an electrical charge will set off dynamite, so the idea of *cessation*—the idea of death, of being dead, eternal sleep, being out of it, stopping the pain—is the spark that ignites the explosive mixture of heightened inimicality-perturbation-constriction. To the desperate person the notion of stopping (or ceasing) seems to provide the perfect solution. It appears to "solve" the problem of the unbearable state of disturbance and isolation. In an inimical-perturbed-constricted person, once the idea of cessation crosses into consciousness, the suicidal act has begun. That idea of cessation—that you can be free of all your problems, get out of this mess, cancel your debts, release yourself from this anguish, stop this disease—is the turning point in the suicidal drama.

Now let us see how these four components of the suicidal drama actually work their ways in two real cases.

One damp and dismal November day a few years ago, a twenty-five-year-old woman, in a state of panic and confusion, jumped from a fifth-floor balcony in a large midwestern metropolitan hospital. She landed on a small grassy knoll, the only such spot in an acre of solid macadam and cement paving. Miraculously, she lived, although she sustained several severe fractures of both legs, ruptures of several internal organs and contusions and abrasions. There was not a scratch on her face; not one of her fingernails was broken.

About a week before, she had ingested a potentially lethal number of sleeping pills, had been discovered by a neighbor and brought to the hospital, had her stomach pumped out in the emergency room and then was moved to a hospital room for further recovery. Unfortunately, her husband refused to accept responsibility for her. He would not approve any medical procedures and he would not pay for her treatment. Further, he told her that he would not permit her to return to their home. On hearing this news, she became agitated and depressed and decided that she had to do *something* to resolve her predicament. She felt overwhelmed by feelings of helplessness and hopelessness. Her "solution" was to kill herself by jumping.

About a week after her suicidal act, I was asked by her resident physician to see her in consultation. I then saw her many times. What follows is a verbatim segment from an exchange that I had with her, together with my comments analyzing some underlying psychological themes.

Shneidman. Then what happened?

T. Well, after that I was out of danger [from the overdose] and they pretty much let me wander around the hospital as I pleased. The next day there was some question about my husband letting me return home, because he thought I was going to make another attempt and he couldn't bear to live with that. And everything was just all up in the air—it was sort of like, well, you go and find a place to stay, and there was no place for me to stay. I don't know anyone here and so it turned out that I was going to be staying in some sort of welfare kind of arrangement which was going to be fixed by the social worker.

Note the mounting despair—like that of a trapped animal. I wonder if her imagery of everything being "up in the air" had anything to do with her choice of method of escape.

S. So you felt at that point rejected by everyone.

T. Yeah. . . . All of a sudden there I was out in the middle of nowhere without any money, and my husband wasn't going to let me come back to the house and I was desperate. And then I went into a terrible state.

The active withdrawal of support by a key "significant other" plunges her even deeper into a state of despair.

S. What did your husband say to you?

T. Well, he said . . . he kept saying, "I'm not going to let you know, I'm going to keep you on tenterhooks. You should learn what it's like to wait and to have patience." So that at this point I was supposed to be making these arrangements myself. I could barely even speak, you know. The social worker was calling various agencies and then turning the telephone over to me so I could tell my story and I could barely remember my name, let alone my date of birth or anything like that. And I thought, My God in heaven, I can hardly even . . . and I was not functioning at all and these people are going to throw me into the street. And I didn't want to go to a psychiatric ward because I was really frightened that I would wind up—that I would possibly have a psychotic episode or something like that.

Here is heightened perturbation, bordering on panic.

S. Had that happened to you before?

T. Almost, yes.

S. Had you had a neuropsychiatric hospitalization?

T. Yes.

S. We'll talk more about that, but not at this moment.

T. And . . . I was so desperate, I felt, My God, I can't face this thing, going out, and being thrown out on the street. And everything was like a terrible sort of whirlpool of confusion. And I thought to myself, There's only one thing I can do, I just have to lose consciousness. That's the only way to get away from it. The only way to lose consciousness, I thought, was to jump off something good and high.

> *Very high perturbation: the phrase "whirlpool of confusion" says it perfectly. Two dangerous and key elements appear:* (a) *constricted dichotomous thinking (*"only *one thing I can do*"; "only *way to lose consciousness*"*); and* (b) *the idea of cessation: to stop the flow of unbearable anguish.*

S. Then what happened?
T. I just figured I had to get outside, but the windows were all locked. So I managed to get outside.
S. How did you do that?
T. I just slipped out. No one saw me. And I got to the other building by walking across that catwalk thing, sure that someone would see me, you know, out of all those windows. The whole building is made of glass.

> *Here is sharp* ambivalence. *There is still the hope for intervention and rescue ("sure that someone would see me* [and stop me]*") during the very moments she is moving to her death.*

S. You were in a hospital gown then?
T. Yes. And I just walked around until I found this open staircase. As soon as I saw it, I just made a beeline right up to it. And then I got to the fifth floor and everything just got very dark all of a sudden, and all I could see was this balcony. Everything around it just blacked out. It was just like a circle. That was all I could see, just the balcony . . . and I went over it.

> *Here is a tragic but explicit (and almost perfect) gut-level description of what psychic constriction really is.*

S. What did you do?

T. I climbed over it and then I just let go. *(Sobbing)* I was so desperate. Just desperation. And the horribleness and the quietness of it. The quiet. Everything became so quiet. There was no sound. And I sort of went into slow motion as I climbed over that balcony. I let go and it was like I was floating. I blacked out. I don't remember any part of the fall. Just . . . just going. I don't remember crying or screaming. I think I was panting from the exertion and the strain of running up all those stairs. And then, when I woke up, I was having a dream, which seemed very weird. At that point I was in an intensive care unit and I was looking at the patterns on the ceiling. . . .

The description of the falling is of keen interest. Time is stopped. There is no kaleidoscopic passing of her life in review—that notion may be a myth. She blacked out and has no memory of her fall and impact.

This nightmare took place five years ago. Now, a few years later, she has recovered both physically and mentally. She has divorced her husband, moved to another state, found a rewarding job, tells people that her slight limp is the result of a terrible automobile accident and writes me messages filled with hope and good cheer. She now believes that her desperate act—"when I committed suicide"—has somehow completely drained off her acutely self-destructive impulses and that she will never again need to resort to that kind of behavior to solve whatever problems her life might present to her.

I agree; I am almost sure that she will never commit suicide. Although hers was a very lethal suicidal act, it needs to be understood in terms of both what led up to it and what followed. The causes of any suicidal event can never be fully fathomed, but we can easily see here the presence of many stressful pressures—within herself, from her usual social environment (especially in her marriage) and from her immediate there-and-then life stresses—which are now in her past.

There is some logic to her recovery—the continued emotional support of her mother, the break with her husband and, she avers, my frequent therapeutic contacts with her—but in addition, there is some magic. It seems to me that her psychological recovery can also be due to her belief that by expiation and fortuitous survival, she has (in terms of her own psychology) acquired the "right to live"—and more than that, the right to assume a sane personality and the right to aspire to live with sanity and her fair share of happiness.

A few years ago I conducted a two-day symposium on suicide prevention at a university other than my own. At the noon break, several people came up to speak with me, among them a very pretty young woman in her early twenties. Her mode of dress was arresting, almost striking. She was wearing an attractive white blouse with a lace choker collar buttoned at her throat and long sleeves with lace at the wrists, and a long, floor-length flowered skirt. She said that she had to talk to me privately.

When we were alone for a few minutes, she undid the buttons at her wrists and a few buttons at her collar to show me that she was lividly scarred on both arms and on her neck and chest. She had, she told me, immolated herself. She asked if she could write to me about it and if so, would I respond to her? I said that she might and that I would—but she never did write to me. However, about a year after that, when I was again lecturing in that general area—in another state, some few hundred miles from the first site—there she was again. She told me that she simply had not been able to bring herself to write. Could she talk to me on tape? Yes, of course. O.K., then, she would try to get a recorder. Let me, I said, send you a small recorder and a dozen tapes—which I did when I returned to my own university.

Some months went by and there was no word. One day, for reasons that I cannot now explain, I became concerned about her welfare and began to worry about her. Finally, I attempted to talk to her by long-distance telephone. I discovered that her number had just recently been disconnected. I then telephoned the chief of police of the small town where she lived to ask him about her whereabouts and her welfare. He told me that she had died just a few days before. The very next day several completed tapes arrived in the mail, and a few days later the recorder was returned by some unknown person.

Except for all dates, personal names (except my own) and place names—as well as some slight shifting in the order of materials and several minor deletions—the text is reproduced exactly as she spoke it.

> It's time for me to begin these tapes again. I have already done these a few times but I haven't been very happy with how they've turned out, so now I'm redoing them again.
>
> > *Here is an example of what I have called the post-self. Most people are extremely interested in their reputations, the ways in which they will be remembered or how they will "live on" after they are dead. Of course, this young woman was not dying when she made the comments, but nevertheless the general point that people are interested in the way in which they will be regarded after they die is still valid.*
>
> My name is Beatrice Kern and I discussed with Dr. Shneidman to do the tapes on an incident of my trying to immolate myself a few years ago. It's just about the anniversary again, it brings back memories by all means.
>
> I guess I should begin and tell you of the incident itself. I'll try to make it as explicit as possible and as pictorial as possible of

what I remember of what occurred that evening. I had been depressed for some months, from probably as early almost as August up until December. I seemed to be able to get out of the depression off and on but I really didn't feel any happiness or any good feelings about myself. I believe in October or November I had attempted suicide. I took an overdose of NoDoz and aspirin, I believe, and I thought I would have heart failure, which I didn't. I was just very, very sick and at that time I did leave a note and I remember being very, very upset.

What we see here are clear indications of elevated perturbation: depression, self-depreciation, a suicide attempt and the feeling of being disturbed.

My roommate and I were living together and I left this note saying, Don't look for me, come into the bedroom later on in the evening and there will be a surprise for you. And I remember that she came into the bedroom, obviously because she was enticed to do so, and of course I wasn't dead, I was just very ill. And at that time—this was either October or November—she was pushing me and had actually made an appointment for me to see a mental health worker because at that time I think she realized that I did need help. But I declined the offer and made some silly excuse of why I couldn't go and I never did go.

Well, then, that takes me up to December and things weren't going well for me: job, social life, personal life, and there were some precipitating factors which probably I should discuss. These were about what had happened before that. Early in December I had dinner with a gentleman, a gentleman who wanted to be engaged to me at one time but I had declined his engagement ring. And I had a dinner engagement with him. He had come one hundred miles to see me. He was still in love with me in many ways. I wasn't at that time in love with him and it was a somewhat nice evening but in some ways it was kind of unhappy for me. There was something I wanted to resolve and it was something I wanted to get rid of at the time. And this was early December and at that time he and I had discussed that I could not go home at Christmas time, which was making me terribly unhappy because I wanted to go home so very badly. He was making arrangements so that I could go home with him and be at his home at Christmas and he was very delighted that I would be with him for the Christmas holidays.

However, I was not very happy about it. I had made the arrangements but it was just not something that I wanted to do. I had discussed with my mother that I had wanted to go home very badly and I was hurting very badly but she kept telling me that it would cost too much money, thirty dollars for the bus ticket to go home, it was not worth it because I would be coming home to go to school in February anyway, and I could wait until then and that it wasn't necessary for me to make this extra trip home. And I couldn't explain to her that I really had mixed feelings. I didn't want to go home to go to school there, for one thing, and second of all, I just wanted to be home at Christmas time in a protected environment and I was very upset that I had to make other arrangements.

> *The deteriorating relationship with her gentleman friend and the unsatisfactory relationship with her mother are aspects of her inimical (partially) self-destructive life style. Note also her feelings of worthlessness and abandonment.*

Another facet of the burning I think that should be mentioned is that my father died. He was accidentally shot in the chest when I was sixteen and I found him and it was in December just before Christmas. Now I've forgotten a bit, but it is almost identically the same day that I tried to immolate myself. Whether there is any correlation between that I don't know. I know I dwelled on the fact before I attempted suicide that it sort of was the right season. It was the time of year when the hurts came out and I had some bad feelings for my father and it just seemed like it all fit together. He died then, and I would die then. And my grandmother also had died of a stroke at Christmas time a few years back, so Christmas in our family is kind of a sad time of year, it's not really very happy and for me especially that Christmas was really not going to be very happy and I kind of added to it.

> *Although suicide does* not *run in families (in the sense that a tendency to it is inherited), it is also true that the suicide of a parent is a heavy psychological legacy to carry. Also, her account raises the issue of "anniversary suicides." They do occur (on both a conscious and an unconscious level), but they are relatively infrequent. This is one of those rare occurrences.*

I have to discuss more the way my father died and how I was involved in it. I saw a psychiatrist and it all came out that I really did love my father. I really thought I hated him. I was very upset with him but he was dead and it came out, I really do think I loved him.

> *An important fact of psychological life is ambivalence—simultaneously feeling opposite feelings toward the same person, like loving* and *hating one's father.*

I just wasn't mature enough or able to accept the fact that he couldn't accept love from a child. And he was having problems himself. It was a very poor relationship and it was dissolved before I understood. I'd like to talk a little bit about how my father died. In some ways it's quite important and also I've resolved it in some ways. I was sixteen and I was going to high school.

My mother didn't get up when I went to school because I was the only one at home and there was really no reason for her to get up. So I went out to the garage to get the car and I was scared to go in. I just opened the door, I recall, but I just couldn't force myself to go in and I just had this great feeling that my father was dead. Now, whether I wished him dead I don't know, but I just had this feeling. I felt very uncomfortable and very nervous inside. So I went back into the house and I walked through the house except for his bedroom.

My mother and father slept in separate bedrooms. My father came and went as he pleased. He would be gone for maybe two or three days at a time and we wouldn't know where he'd be and it wasn't unusual that he would be gone. We would never ask him where he would go because we would always get a snide remark that it was none of our business and to let him be. So we had learned not to ask him. And so I don't know why, it just was odd to me that he hadn't been home. And I woke my mother up and I told her that I thought something was really wrong. I thought something was really wrong. I thought my father was dead and that he was in his room. And she said, "Oh, don't be silly, I'll go in there with you." And so she did. And we walked in the room and there he was lying on the floor. There he was, frozen stiff in a pool of blood.

My mother immediately went into the kitchen and started calling people. She wasn't sure of really what happened. And what did happen was that he was cleaning an old revolver at his desk, and it was a faulty gun, it was a really old gun and not well kept up. And it had fallen over on the seat and caught on a little tab or something on the seat and shot him in the head as he was trying to catch it.

He died instantly, from what we understand from the coroner's report, and it was proven that it was not suicide. However, he had threatened suicide and he had talked about it with my aunt, his sister, and with my mother and we were all quite aware of it, so my mother was quite sure that he had committed suicide. Well, my aunt who lives very close, my father's sister, she came down and was with us and at that time she stood and she told me that I had killed my father, that he had committed suicide because of me.

My father and I had been into a row earlier in the fall, but my aunt really stunned me by saying that I had killed my father. So it was something that was put on me. Now, whether I believed it or not, that I had played a part in it, I really don't know, but I know that I was greatly hurt by it. It was just hard for me to take.

It is hardly necessary to underline the harmful effect of

> *such an ugly remark. One can only speculate about the aunt's hostility and why she would make Beatrice the target of it.*

After that I did not want any part of her, and I made up my mind I would get her. I would annihilate her in some way, shape or form, before too long. And then I came to the attitude that it really wasn't worth it, that she was hurting badly enough, and I dropped my hate. And so my father was dead and there were all sorts of repercussions about his death. It was so violent and it was so quick and it was so hard to accept. It was just kind of unreal. This row that we had been into earlier in the fall was that my father was saying that I was breaking him, I was costing him way too much money and that he couldn't afford to keep me and I couldn't understand it. I was very upset by it and I had made arrangements that I would go away and I would live in a foster home and work and go to high school. But my mother wouldn't allow me to. She said that I had to stay at home, where I belonged, that I couldn't leave in spite of whatever. But my father had been trying to push me out for quite some time and I had supported myself quite well for clothes and school supplies and different articles that I had earned through baby-sitting, through waitressing, but he and I just weren't getting along at that time. We were having quite some difficulties and I know he wasn't communicating in any way. So there it left me with my father dead.

Also, the other factor that was existing at that time with my father was that he was calling me a whore, that I was a, you know, loose lady because I was dating and that I was screwing around. And the fact was that I had actually gone with only a few guys at the time I was sixteen, and I had slept with no one. And I think after he died, my way of getting back was that he died in December and on January first I made sure I lost my virginity.

> *The unconscious psychodynamic implications of her losing her virginity at this time—touching on her need for autonomy, revenge, grief, unconscious desire for reunion*

with the deceased loved one—all indicate how enormously complicated behavior can be.

My mother is a very dominant person. Yet she'll say always that she really didn't want to be that strong, but I think that's a bunch of bullshit. She's always been domineering. She's always been aggressive and she didn't really allow my father to stand up. However, I think he had his problems too and he really couldn't. So I don't know, it's six of one and half dozen of the other. As I see it honestly, if I evaluate it myself—like I've asked my uncle who knew my father way back when, and he said he was a very nice man—I wish I could have known that niceness, because I think I missed out. My mother kind of turned him into being hateful in a way, I think. She pushed him that way, and he was kind of sad.

And there was always just a conflict, and this confiict was money. My mother is very manipulating with money but she is quite generous in taking care of your needs at various times. She uses money as a weapon, but my father, he was just very miserly. He thought it was a big deal if once a month he threw you a dollar. He would just literally throw it at you. It was just a real smart-alecky thing—like he was doing you such a favor. But he was such a kid himself that it was just sad. He worked so damned hard and his life was really unfulfilled—very, very unhappy in many ways.

My mother took good care of him physically. She always had meals for him, she always had clothes for him, everything was done for him, but she was so mean to him in lots of ways. Like I know one time my father and I had gotten into a row. We had gone to town and it was the deal that my father would drink beer and usually he was pretty cheap so he would say, If you have enough money I'll take you to town and we'll buy beer and we'll split it. So he'd use my money to buy beer for him. And we'd gone to town and he'd got himself a beer and I don't know how many he'd had before that. This was earlier in the year that I was sixteen, and I had wanted a car and I had chosen one and I had wanted it quite badly and I decided that I needed one terribly bad and I was a bit spoiled, I guess, and wanted my own way. And he and I were talking about it and he sort of turned, his eyes just got black and he just got into this rage and he just hollered at me, You're just like your mother, and he was saying such ugly things about me, I don't recall. His eyes were so black I was really frightened. I just thought he was going to kill me and he hit me across the face and I tried to get out of the car he was driving and I couldn't, he held me in.

And all of a sudden after he hit me he calmed down just like that. It was just like a peace came over him. He released his anger or something and he was apologizing over and over and over again and by this time I was becoming quite hysterical and crying and just mad, madder than hell that how dare he strike me, and he kept pleading with me not to tell my mother, Don't tell your mother, and of course I did. I went home immediately and told her and she kept him up till three or four in the morning hollering at him, how stupid to do that to the child over nothing. She would carry on things from way far past, things that had happened years ago, and held a grudge. This is how she dealt with him and she just was an unbelievable fighter. It's just an ugly fight. And yet if he defended himself, which many times he did, he was just as nasty too and he would call her all dirty different names too. So the situation was kind of sad. And I have to admit that after he was dead, after a period of time my feelings about it were that I was sort of happy for him in a way. That his misery was kind of gone and I think he lived a sad enough life as it was. I don't think he was very happy and maybe it was better for all of us in some ways, it eased our tensions. . . .

A few years back my mother and I went out in the country and, I don't know, I have this thing about cemeteries, I guess. I really like old cemeteries and this relates mostly to my father and it was kind of putting things together for me, it's an incident that was really important to me.

> *Note here—as we shall in other cases in this book—the special appeal of the cemetery. It seems to represent a sanctuary: the special peace and protection given by the dead, who never scold and never hate.*

We were in this old cemetery and what was interesting and unique about this cemetery is that it was very old and the crosses were wooden and they were rotting away and they were waving in the breeze and they were just—just gorgeous really, just really fine classic gravestones and the daisies were blooming and the grasses were blooming on the graves and growing tall and the breeze was blowing and I was just so impressed by the earthiness of it and life, of this part of death. I really thought it was nifty and I looked over a ways and in the newer part of the cemetery here the grass was clipped. It was kept well and it was clipped short and it looked so stilted, so guilty. And I was thinking that in one of these older graves finally there is no man to control at all. It seems like in life man tries to control when death occurs also. Even though we can't control our own death, we try to control our feelings about other people's deaths. And when God or whoever, in quotes—Nature, let's say, Mother Nature—was able to take over, she said it so much better, she was able to do it gracefully and graciously and time it in this circle that life and death, this body in the earth created new life and it was put together, it was a completed circle. Whereas when you see the clipped graves, the grass, it's almost sad, it's almost a guilt feeling. It's almost like people have to hang on. They have to control because it's their way of saying that they still care and I just thought, Wow, you know, they don't allow those people to die. They don't allow them to complete the circle of life and death, and I think I put it together for my father, that he went back to the soil and it was O.K. At last I felt good about it, that it was O.K., it was something I could never change and it's something I don't ever want to change and I don't regret it. It's something that happened and I accept it now. My mother has never really accepted his death, I don't think. I mean he is dead in all ways, but she hated him and she despised him and she was going to leave him and she fought with him. But in his death, he holds her. Had she left him before, she could have left with a clean slate and I think she actually would have left us children too, but as it was, he died on her suddenly and unexpectedly and so now she hangs on for dear life to many of the memories of things that he liked and things that he hung on to. A prime example of that is that she isolates herself and works like a knothead. I feel it's kind of unhealthy for her to be so isolated all the time and working so hard at her age. It's not right, but that's the way she is.

> *This long monody reminds one of the poetic line "Death, easeful death . . ." She seems to reify Death and view Death as a comforter and as a natural part of life.*

Well, then, I guess I can bring you up to that December, the date of the incident.

> *Without knowing it, she uses just the right word: "incident." It is a neutral, nonjudgmental word, like "act," "event," "occurrence." It is different from "gesture," "threat" or "attention-getting behavior," which are all judgmental terms—and to be avoided. The immolation is better described as an incident, event, act or deed, than by the words "attempted suicide" or "committed suicide." It was a suicidal incident—albeit of extremely high lethality.*

I remember being very unhappy that week. Things were not working out. I was not working, I recall. It was cold. I was without money. Friends were not helping me a whole lot. I was not getting along well with them. However, I really wasn't fighting with them. But I had various friends that I did know and it just seemed like they just really didn't have time for me and I was hurting very badly inside and it just, just was an overwhelming desire, I guess, to die.

> *". . . an overwhelming desire to die" is an example of the idea of cessation—the spark that sets off a suicidal incident.*

And I know I debated about this death, I'm sure, around two to three months, if I recall. I had planned and planned and planned and of course the attempt earlier in October or November did not work out, so it just sort of added to it. It frustrated me even further that I wasn't able to die. So what was going through my mind is that I would burn myself.

I knew that I had read somewhere in the newspaper that the people in Vietnam, I believe, committed suicide by burning themselves. It was just a sure deal that they would die. And I think it went through my mind that this was how I was going to do it. And part of the reason was because I knew it was a sure deal.

> *". . . sure deal," synonymous with "certainty" (as opposed to* any *degree of uncertainty), repeated twice in the above paragraph, reflects the constriction of her thought processes and tunnel vision at that time.*

I knew that I would not live and I knew that these people just died. There was no way of surviving. So this is why I made the decision and I sort of dwelled on it. It was just something that I thought and thought and thought about a lot and I really hadn't picked a day at all. It was sort of something that I was kind of waiting out.

Well, on that day I don't recall getting up early in the morning, but knowing myself, probably I didn't. There was really probably no reason for me to. But by this time I had gotten most of my things together and I imagine I hadn't gotten my things together all in that one day, I'm sure I had worked on my things way before that, a few days at least before that. What I was getting together were my books, my clothing, the things that I owned, the things that were mine, my personal possessions, the little odds and ends, knickknacks that I had collected, some paintings and different ceramic items. Things that I had collected, things that were meaningful to me. And everything was very well organized and I remember, later on in the afternoon, everything was very well put together and I remember being semi-tearful and just very down in the mouth but I had energy. I had energy that I could do things. I was able to function.

> *Putting one's affairs in order is one of the typical behaviors or clues that people give before they commit suicide.*

It was probably between six and seven o'clock when this all came about. I had been quite upset, but I wasn't crying. I wasn't taking any action on it, but I just really wasn't feeling very well.

I was just feeling very bad and sad for myself and very sorry for myself. Things just were not happening, things were not working out. At six o'clock this woman, Mrs. Brown, called me and she had been drinking some. Mrs. Brown, in relation to me, was the mother of an ex-boyfriend of mine, but actually at the time I considered him a boyfriend and somebody that I thought I cared a whole lot about and worried a whole lot about and wanted him to love me ever so badly, but he didn't. He was twenty-six years old at the time. I was nineteen. He was going to school full-time along with working a full-time job. And he more or less played me for laughs, had used me, had taken advantage of me sexually and otherwise. I thought I had been good to him and I had given him all, all my feelings, all my hopes, all my desires, all my dreams, and yet he sort of laughed at it. He sort of took advantage of it and walked away, like, Well, that's how it is, sweetie, that's how life is. Some people are takers and some people are givers and you're a giver and I'm a taker. At the time I didn't really know how to cope with it. I was very, very upset and was almost bitter in some ways but wanted him so badly. By this time in December he was already dating other people and I was well aware that he had been dating other girls but that still didn't impress upon me that he no longer had any cares for me.

So this particular evening his mother had called me and she was going on and on and on about a Christmas present that a girl friend had given him. It was a watch, a gold watch that he was so impressed with and felt it was the most beautiful gift that he could ever receive. And what was going through my mind at that time was that I feel that I, and even now I feel like I am a very generous person and I would give almost anybody anything that would make them very happy monetarily and I would give them almost anything feeling-wise, anything of myself. And I had wanted to give him a lovely, lovely Christmas present and through the back of my mind I had set my goals for it to be a stereo that I had wanted to give him. But of course, I had no money or very little money, just mere sustenance, that's about all. I didn't have anything. That I really couldn't consider giving him a stereo in any way and that was really breaking my heart.

Now, if I had the money I don't know if I would have bought him a stereo or not. But I could not give him really anything that was really very meaningful because of lack of money. So I had bought him a record called *Good Night Sweetheart,* which was meaningful to me in a way, but it was a very sad record and this was all that I could offer him. And I knew at that time it would not have been impressive to him at all. And Mrs. Brown was going on about this watch and about how great it was and how her son felt so much and thought so much of this girl. And I started sobbing on the phone. I was sobbing for myself then and feeling that I really was a nothing. I really had nothing to offer. I could in no way compete. I could in no way ever share a love with this guy and I was just very broken-hearted and I was very upset and I started to sob.

And she finally sensed that I was very upset and she said, what was wrong, and I wouldn't tell her and she went on and on and asked me what was wrong. And she said, Well, why don't you come over and maybe you'll feel better, come over, I don't want you crying, and I said, Oh, no, I'd be all right, and I sort of contained myself. I felt a bit better for a second. So finally we terminated the conversation.

Well, almost immediately she had her husband call me. And he had a pet name for me, which at this time I don't recall, but he called me by the pet name and he was kind of a cute little man in a way, and he pleaded for me to come over because he knew I was upset. And to pacify him I said certainly, I would be over in fifteen minutes. It was like the straw that broke the camel's back. I sort of had had enough piled up on me that I really couldn't handle it.

> *Here is an accumulation of psychological insults too painful for her to bear: To be told by your mother-in-law-never-to-be that your ex-lover (who has rejected you) was given a glorious gift that you couldn't afford, and then to have your "cute little" father-in-law-never-to-be call you by some pet name is just too much.*

This was all that I could take. It was just enough. There was no more that I wanted to hear. There was no more that I wanted to see. There was no more that I wanted to live and I knew that my *only* out was death. And at this time I made the decision, that evening about six o'clock.

> *Here is a perfect and so very sad example of constriction. The words "all," "no more," and especially that frightening word "only," are the keys to it. When she says, "my only out was death," she need hardly have added the next sentence: ". . . at this time I made the decision . . ."*

I had no interruptions. There was nobody to hold me back in any way, that I would change my mind that this is what I had to do. I did go, I did put on a nylon bathrobe, and the thought that was going through my mind at the time, I remember, was that I couldn't possibly ruin my clothes because that would be very selfish. Somebody certainly could use them other than myself even though I knew I wouldn't be around. But I couldn't ruin my items that would be useful to other people, so I put on a very thin nylon bathrobe and I did have a brassiere on and underpants and I put on an old pair of loafers that I did have. It was cold outside and I did put on a coat then at the time.

I had an electric toaster that I had to return to some friends' house which was a few blocks away. So I got into the car and at the time took a jar, a glass gallon jug, and took it with me along with the toaster and I remember kind of shaking when I was getting the jug because I think I was a bit afraid. I was a bit nervous that I had made the decision. I was kind of scared, almost like I had to do it. It was something I was kind of forced into in a way. But yet it was something I knew I had to accomplish. So I took the toaster to these friends' house and they were home. I remember just walking in and walking through the house and by this time I was sobbing again. And not one word was said to me by these people. I think there were around four people in the house. And I just walked through the house, put the toaster on the kitchen table and walked right out. And nobody touched my arm, nobody said what's wrong, nobody even gestured, and I think it upset me even more that this was sort of the end. Nobody really reached out for me in any way and I think at that time I really must have been reaching out. I must have been saying, You know I am really upset. I am really having problems. But at that second nobody responded.

> *I have puzzled much over this bizarre event. It seems to me to read almost like a scene out of the theater of the absurd, something that Genêt or Beckett or Ionesco might have written. There are other possible scenarios that I wonder about: Did it actually happen this way? Were her friends drunk or stoned? Had she done something like this several times before and were they fed up with her? But the fact is—like the jumper—she was keenly ambivalent: she was on the way to her death and,* at the same time, *she was reaching out for help and for intervention and rescue. No matter how it is read, it is a poignant and harrowing scene.*

I remember getting back in the car and feeling ever so much alone because these were my friends and even they did not care, even they did not want to share my sadness, and even they wanted no part of that part of me. When I was happy, it was fine, but if I was sad it did not make any difference and they didn't realize the extent of my thoughts or my feelings.

I got back into the car and I drove to a gas station and bought a gallon of gas. And no questions were asked. And I took the gallon of gas in my car and I drove back to my apartment building, and I parked the car.

I think at this time I went into the apartment building and took the gas with me and decided that I would burn myself in the apartment building. I really hadn't made complete plans as it was, right then. Well, what happened to me then is that I decided since I couldn't destroy my clothes because I had to let my clothes go to other people, I really couldn't destroy the building because I thought the building might catch on fire and I couldn't be responsible for other people's possessions being ruined. I couldn't do that to other people. I felt that I had always tried my best not to hurt other people and I really couldn't hurt other people in that way. I only wanted to hurt and kill myself. There were no feelings of wanting to take it out on anybody else. So at that time I left my coat in the building and made the decision that I would go and burn myself in the car. My car was parked out in front.

I did take a book of matches with me. And it seemed like I moved slowly at that time. It wasn't really quick movement, physical movement, it seemed like I was moving like in slow motion almost. I was making these decisions and I don't remember things going through my mind or even thinking of my sadness or the things that were breaking my heart. It was kind of like the end of things that I was thinking about, that I would be no more. I would hurt no more. It was going to be good, it was going to be something that was going to fulfil me. I was going to be strong and be able to perform something. It was sort of like slow motion. A lot of things were going though my head but I remember not sobbing at this time. I was not upset any longer in that way. I was not releasing it by tears.

> *The change in the rate at which time seems to move—"slow motion"—is certainly similar to the jumper's description: "And I sort of went into slow motion as I climbed over that balcony." Time, at these moments, seems to stand still.*

I remember sitting in the car for just a second and it was sort of like a blank in my mind. I don't remember thinking about a whole lot of things, but I felt very calm. I felt very good. I felt kind of a hush over my body that it was going to be O.K.

> *What is noteworthy here is that having made the decision, she is at peace with herself. In the previous paragraph she said: "I would hurt no more." And here she utters one of her memorable phrases: "I felt a kind of hush over my body."*

And I remember then pouring the gasoline first over the front seat and myself and then over the back seat and just sprinkling it and of course over myself to a great extent, and I laid the jar then on the seat. Well, then what I proceeded to do is I got the matches out, and even then no thoughts went through my head at all of the pain that it was going to entail, the misery, the hurt, any of that. It amazes me now that I really didn't think those thoughts. I guess I don't know why I didn't think that burns would really hurt, but none of that went through my head. It just felt good. It was the first time, in fact, that I had felt at peace, that I wasn't hurting inside. At times before that it felt like I had just been stabbed and was bleeding and people were just watching me bleed, seeing the blood flow, and almost laughing, saying, ha, ha, that's your problem. And for once it seemed like I had taken care of my problems and no one had to watch my sores anymore and that my pain would just go away. It was not going to exist anymore, especially my mental pain.

Well, I opened the match book and struck one match and it would not light. It was soaked with gas and I kind of sort of smiled to myself, thinking, Well, I'll have to try a second one, because the first one just would not light. And I remember very slowly striking the second one and it did strike and it did light. And at that second the fumes ignited, just a tremendous explosion. It was an overwhelming sound. The noise was terribly loud. It was almost a gush. It was like a very heavy pressure being pressed against my body and then immediately I felt the pain. I felt a sudden surge of just cringing, and as I looked at my burn scars now I must have flexed my whole body in an almost protective position. But the pain was unbelievable. It was just over my whole body. It was just such a sudden pressure of heat and flame and it just really hurt and the noise was so loud.

> *Again, a pathetic example of constricted thinking: not to think that burning oneself would hurt, which she herself acknowledges: "It amazes me now that I really didn't think those thoughts."*

I remember holding my breath because I couldn't stand the smell of the gasoline. So I did hold my breath, which I understand did help in saving me because had my lungs been burned, I would have been dead. But I did hold my breath because I could not stand the smell of gasoline, and I did stand the surge of heat. Well, by the second surge of heat—it surged once and I don't know how many seconds that entailed, but the second surge—oh, God, oh, God, the pain by this time was just so magnanimous [*sic*] I just couldn't stand it any longer and I was almost reaching for the door to push myself out because at that moment it wasn't very peaceful and it was hurting so badly, but I don't recall crying out. I don't think I screamed, I don't think I hollered. It was just silent except for this ignition [*sic*] of the car. It was just so, so loud.

There were two to three people who were across the street and they saw the car ignite and they came rushing over, I believe. I didn't see them. But they came rushing over and they opened the door very fast. This was the second surge of heat and they pulled me out and they rolled me on the ground as fast as they could and they were, I remember them, shouting and were very excited. But they were rolling me on the ground and the grass was very damp and cold and it was wintery and I didn't have many clothes on by this time. And I remember, at that time, looking down at myself and I was just shocked. I saw this skin, just layers of skin hanging off my arms and off my chest. It just seemed like huge triangles, like pie crusts, just hanging off of me, of this singed, curled skin and it was almost yellowish. And by this time I think I was a bit upset about it but I wasn't sure. These people are immediately saying, What a horrible accident, what a horrible accident, and I'm hollering, saying, But it wasn't. I wanted to die. I wanted to die. And I was almost frustrated with them for saying such things. And in the meantime they began to carry me, one took my arms and the other took my legs.

Well, in the meantime they did carry me across the street and I'm still extremely angry and I'm hollering, It was not an accident, I wanted to die, why didn't you let me die, here you are interfering. And they're just shocked, they're just in utter amazement that this had happened and totally unaccepting and they laid me on the carpet in their living room and I'm able to glance down at this time, however, I don't try to move, I don't try to get up, I can hardly see, just this charred body, what little I could see

> was just very charred. Immediately, the ambulance came and also the police came and I remember them putting me on the stretcher and the ride to the hospital and I remember not saying anything and I remember trying to joke with them or something because they looked so grim. They looked not knowing quite how to respond to me, yet I was awake and I remember trying to think of a joke or trying to be flippant about it, but I didn't have those feelings to be flippant.
>
> And so we went into the emergency room and there was all this flutter, all kinds of people. It seemed like just on and on people and I was just talking with somebody, they were asking my name and where I lived and various things about me and I remember being able to answer and then also I started in on the fact that I wanted a cigarette and I wanted a drink of water. I needed a cigarette very badly and a drink of water. I was very thirsty. I was very dry and I even at that time didn't really try to move. Well, immediately the surgeon seemed to show up. He starts cutting the clothes off me, the nylon that had been melted into me and there didn't seem like there was very much of it but he did cut instead of trying to take anything off, he just cut it off and laid it apart. And I'm still hollering that I want a cigarette and I want a drink of water and I will be all right and all this business, and he's saying, When you get better you can have anything you want, but shut up now, you're very sick right now. And I don't think it even dawned on me how badly I was burned at the time. It was just amazing. Well, I remember him cutting things off of me and I remember them starting to treat me in some ways but I just vaguely remember them putting bandages on me, vaguely. Then it seemed like it just all went black.

Of course, following the burning she remained in the hospital for several months. There were a half-dozen operations for skin grafts (each with a general anesthetic), hundreds of sessions with physical therapists, and encounters with a hospital nun who berated her for having grievously sinned by attempting suicide.

The forerunners to suicide in her life are not hard to find.

There is a whole list of them: a quarrelsome family; her being deprecated as a child by her parents; her identifying with the rejections by her father and her aunt and incorporating these ideas so that she then rejected herself; her being jilted and her subsequent declining self-esteem; and more. The precipitating events can also be listed: her mother's refusal to let her come home; parental affection from a man who could never be her father-in-law; a total lack of any response from her friends to her last cry for help; and a spiraling down and constriction of her inner world. She wanted to end it all—without even considering that being burned to death would be excruciatingly painful.*

She died about three years after the immolation. The facts about her death are these: Two days before her death she saw a doctor—who had been told that her burn scars were the result of an automobile accident—complaining of a sore throat. During that visit her throat was cultured, acute tonsillitis was found and she was placed on an oral medication and was asked to return the following day. When she returned, she complained of some nausea and inability to keep the medication down. The doctor hospitalized her and ordered some intravenous medication for her acute tonsillitis. He visited her at the hospital around 5:00 P.M. In the evening she talked to some friends by telephone. At midnight she reported to the nurse that she was feeling much better. She was found dead in bed at approximately 4:00 A.M. There was no evidence of any struggle.

It was then learned that around two weeks prior to her entering the hospital she had had a flu-like episode and had stayed home from work for a few days. (It was perhaps on these days that she dictated her tapes.) In retrospect, her doctor now believes that the flu-like episode was a coronary attack, and that

*A word of scientific caution: All these items seem to be "necessary" but not "sufficient" causes to explain this suicide. We all know individuals who have suffered what appear to be these same torments and deprivations and who did not commit suicide. So there must be something more.

she died from cardiac arrhythmia. Moreover, the autopsy and toxicological assay revealed neither abnormal stomach contents nor abnormal blood chemistry. I would agree that there was no evidence pointing to suicide. Her death certificate lists the cause of death as "Congestive Heart Failure (4 hours) due to Myocardial Infarction (14 days); also Acute Tonsillitis and Pneumonitis."

Her body was shipped to her home town. Her mother had her cremated.

Both of these documents, in their entirety, are rutters which alert us to some of the jagged shoals and volcanic islands in life's open seas. They warn us whom to avoid in life—rejecting fathers, hostile mothers, spiteful aunts, exploiting lovers, unloving husbands, unresponsive friends, disapproving nurses, etc. Yet they cannot tell us *how* to avoid these calamitous relationships. Rutters and maps need to be supplemented by other instructions—not only "where" and "what," but "how." But it is still important to understand what should have been avoided.

The challenge for each person is to try to make certain that such disastrous elements do not exist in your own life or in the lives of your children and other loved ones. Unfortunately, the facts show that battered children tend themselves to become battering parents and it would seem, by extension, that traumatized and rejected children become traumatizing and rejecting parents. To have examined rutters of several disastrous life voyages and then to continue to proceed through life as though there weren't a guide map in the whole world is a sad commentary, when it happens, on the rigidity of some human personalities.

In addition to the obvious lessons inherent in their content, these two extraordinary accounts, both prepared after a highly lethal suicide act, raise a number of interesting methodological questions. How changed are the accounts by virtue of their having been written *after* the near-fatal event? How different would they have sounded if they had been dictated just *before* the jumping or the immolation?

We know that the act of investigating a phenomenon in nature—the very looking at it (whether under a microscope or by means of a tape recorder)—changes the event or phenomenon, however slightly, from what it would be like in its totally native or unobserved state. This certainly seems to be true in the psychological field, where the presence of the observer changes what is being "observed." But for those of us who are interested in the serious study of suicidal phenomena, there is hardly a way around this dilemma.

Perhaps, then, the records of these two women do not totally reflect what the actual suicidal state is like because they were made after the event, after the survival, after some reflection. But they do give us a tremendous amount of information compared with no records at all. They are perhaps as close to the "real thing" as we are likely to come.

These two personal documents are presented neither as representative nor as typical, but simply as examples of what the human spirit, in situations of bewilderment and duress, seeks to communicate, if only to itself. They are simply two voices of death in Everyman's wilderness.

3

Self-Destruction: Suicide Notes and Tragic Lives

> The path to my fixed purpose is laid with iron rails, whereon my soul is grooved to run.
>
> Herman Melville, *Moby Dick* (Chapter 37)

There is probably no description of suicide that contains as much insight in as few words as that found in the opening paragraph of *Moby Dick:* ". . . a damp, drizzly November in my soul." In its essence, that is what most suicide is: a dreary and dismal wintry storm within the mind, where staying afloat or going under is the vital decision being debated. In about one fourth of these occasions where a suicide is going to be committed, the individual will write something about that debate. Those documents—suicide notes—have something of the fascination of a cobra: they catch our eyes, yet we are ever conscious that some serious threat may lurk in them.

As rutters, suicide notes are cryptic maps of ill-advised journeys. A suicide note, no matter how persuasive it seems within its own closed world, is not a model for conducting a life. When one examines suicide notes, one can only shudder to read these testimonials to tortuous life journeys that came to wrecked ends. They fascinate us for what they tell us about the human condition and what they warn us against in ourselves.

My own long-term sustained study of them is admittedly a somewhat arcane pursuit. It would be like someone's contemporary fascination with alchemy, phlogiston or the inheritance of acquired characteristics, or with the notion that the world is flat, or that the earth is the center of the universe, or the proof that Bacon really wrote Shakespeare's plays—all flawed ideas. The difference that may make my obsession with suicide notes seem legitimate is that I know that suicide notes—like the many schizophrenic diaries I have read—are flawed rutters. I have never read a suicide note that I would want to have written.

But what can we actually learn about suicide from suicide notes? In the last twenty-five years, my answers to this question have undergone some radical changes. I have held three different positions on the relationship of suicide notes to suicidal phenomena.

My original view on the value of suicide notes dates from that special day in 1949 when I unexpectedly came across several hundred suicide notes in the vaults of a coroner's office. Since then, almost without a flagging of interest, I have been fascinated with suicide notes as perhaps the best available way of understanding suicidal phenomena. I believed that it was possible to unlock the mysteries of suicidal phenomena by using suicide notes as the keys. When one addresses the question: "Why do people take this trip?" (i.e., commit suicide), one can reasonably look upon suicide notes as psychological rutters and search them for clues as to how the tragic outcome of that life's voyage might have been averted. It would seem that suicide notes, written as they are in the very context of the suicidal act, often within a few minutes of the death-producing deed, would offer a special window into the thinking and the feeling of the act itself. In no other segment of human behavior is there such a close relationship of document to deed.

My subsequent counterreaction to that view was a (somewhat exaggerated) jump to an almost opposite position. In that position I believed that suicide notes, written as they were by individuals in a state of psychological constriction and of truncated and narrowed thinking, could hardly ever—by virtue of the state in which they were composed—be illuminating or even important psychological documents. Admittedly, that point of view had a touch of "overkill" in it.

I now believe that suicide notes, by themselves, are uniformly neither bountiful nor banal, but that they definitely can have a great deal of meaning under certain circumstances, specifically when they are put into the context of the detailed life history of the individual who both wrote the note and committed the act. In those instances—where we have both the suicide note and an extended life history—the note will then illuminate many aspects of the life history, and conversely, the life history can make many key words of the note come alive and take on special meanings that would otherwise have remained hidden or lost. My present view is thus an amalgamation of my two previous views.

To readers who know their philosophy, this process will remind them of the ideas of the German philosopher Georg Wilhelm Friedrich Hegel. Hegel believed that all thought and development of ideas proceeded in a certain way. Specifically, the process begins with an affirmation of an idea (which he called the "thesis"), then it gives way to its opposite (the "antithesis"), and then the two are united by a new idea which combines them (the "synthesis"). This process (which may take minutes or years or decades or centuries), repeated over and over, endlessly, Hegel called the "dialectic." (This idea influenced Friedrich Engels and Karl Marx in their "dialectical materialism.") What has happened over the last quarter century in relation to my own thoughts about suicide notes has unconsciously mirrored some aspects of this basic dialectical process and might be called a "dialectical suicidology."

I

The findings of many previous investigations over the past century—starting with Brierre de Boismont's systematic study in 1856—have been extraordinarily diverse and diffuse. As a whole, these studies of suicide notes tell us that the suicidal person—specifically as compared with the nonsuicidal person—is likely to think in terms of dichotomous logic, separating everything in his world into two mutually exclusive categories (like perfect and nothing, life and death), and to be constricted and focused in his thinking; to think in terms of specific instructions (as opposed to broad or philosophic generalizations), writing to his survivors-to-be as though he were going to be alive to supervise his wishes; to avoid intellectualizing (i.e., to avoid thinking about how he is thinking), dealing more with raw feeling than with rational thought; to be concerned with blaming, both others (the expression of hostility) and oneself (the expression of guilt or shame); and to be concerned with love—the various aspects, nuances and shading of affection, affiliation, devotion and either romantic or erotic love.

The figures vary as to the percentage of individuals who commit suicide who also leave suicide notes, ranging from 15 percent to over 30 percent. Who, among those who commit suicide, writes suicide notes? Except for knowing that note writers and non-note writers are essentially similar in terms of all the major demographic variables—age, race, sex, employment status, marital status, physical condition, history of mental illness, place of suicide and history of previous suicidal attempts—we know very little about the psychology of suicide-note writing. The distinguished suicidologist Erwin Stengel, in his scholarly book *Suicide and Attempted Suicide,* said: "Whether the writers of suicide notes differ in their attitudes from those who leave no notes behind, it is impossible to say. Possibly they differ from the majority only in being good correspondents." That sounds like as reasonable an explanation as any.

Studies of suicide notes have dispelled at least one myth about suicide: that suicidal acts are uniformly motivated by a single formula. Of course, no one commits suicide who is not, in some way and to some heightened extent, intellectually or emotionally distraught, but these perturbations can take the form of the passions of unrequited love, intellectual self-assertion, shame and guilt related to disgrace, the wish to escape from the pain of insanity, the wish to spare loved ones from further anguish, and a sense of inner pride and autonomy connected to one's own fate and the manner of one's own death. All these psychological threads, and more, are found in suicide notes.

Suicidal acts are very complicated psychological events—never mind their social, sociological or anthropological components. "Just" from a psychological point of view, there are many underlying, resonating and sustaining causes (together with a multiplicity of precipitating events) that come together in each suicidal event. Nevertheless, we occasionally find a suicide note in which one particular emotional state will figure so clearly that it will seem to characterize (or at least to dominate) that particular suicidal act. In these cases we are almost beguiled into believing that this single emotion was the sole (if not the primary) cause of the act itself. Here are some examples.

HATE

In the now famous meeting of Freud and others in Vienna in 1910—the only meeting of the psychoanalytic group specifically on the topic of suicide—Wilhelm Stekel enunciated what was to become the orthodox psychoanalytic view. He said: "No one kills himself except as he wishes the death of another."[1] Suicide was seen by the early psychoanalysts primarily as hostility directed toward the ambivalently viewed loved person who had been introjected into one's own unconscious mind—what I have called "murder in the 180th degree."

It is certainly not difficult to find evidence of hostility in contemporary suicide notes that would seem to support this hypothesis. The following hate note is from a most unusual set of suicide notes. Between 1934—the year after Fiorello La Guardia became mayor of New York City and began to reform the police department—and 1940, in a half-dozen years, ninety-three New York City policemen committed suicide. (Only two papers have been written about this strange epidemic.)[2] Among these ninety-three police suicides, nineteen left suicide notes. Here is one of the shortest and one of the angriest, written by a thirty-seven-year-old patrolman who was in a bar waiting for his sergeant, whom he had planned to kill. After a long wait, he wrote this hate-laden note and then shot himself.

> To whom concerned: Goodbye you old prick and when I mean prick you are a prick. Hope you fall with the rest of us, you yellow bastard. May the precinct get along without you.

Love

Currently, most suicidologists believe that suicide is not motivated by hostility alone, but that there are many other emotional states—such as dependency, shame, guilt, fear, despair, frustration, loss of autonomy and especially feelings of hopelessness and helplessness—that can be the basic psychological ingredients of suicide. Love, especially frustrated love, seems to play as great a role in as many cases of suicide as does hate. A young man of thirty-five wrote the following contemporary note:

> My Darling, To love you as I do and live without you is more than I can bear. I love you so completely, wholeheartedly without restraint. I worship you, that is my fault. . . . Without you life is unbearable. This is the best way. This will solve all our problems. . . . If it is possible to love in the hereafter, I will love you even after death. God have mercy on both our souls. He alone knows my heartache and love for you.

Here is a love suicide note from a European woman of the last century who was the daughter of a very famous man. Consider, in the following brief suicide note by Eleanor Marx,[3] the youngest of Karl Marx's three daughters—whose sister also committed suicide—the complicated and overladen meanings of the word "love." One needs to keep in mind her tremendously complicated and psychologically tortured relationship with her famous father. For example, she did not learn until she was an adult that her father had had an illegitimate son by one of the dear friends of the family—and she immediately had to make a close psychological relationship with this person. Also keep in mind that her suicide note is addressed to her lover of several years, an unpredictable person who had had numerous affairs with other women, which she tolerated because she loved him. But there was a last straw which broke her heart. This man, Edward Aveling, had, without telling her, secretly married another woman. For Eleanor, that was the ultimate betrayal and rejection. Her note reads:

> Dear, It will soon be over. My last word to you is the same that I have said during all these long, sad years—love.

She drank prussic acid in her apartment. It is unclear today whether Aveling arranged for her to have the poison or whether there was a suicide pact, from which he fled. What is clear is the ambiguity of that key word, "love." It can be read to mean bitterness, regret, accusation, disappointment, tenderness, nostalgia, impotent rage or helplessness at being duped or traduced.

An important key to suicide is to recognize that its cause is neither love nor hate; rather, it is the simultaneous presence of *both* of them as well as other emotions. This state of being able to experience contradictory emotions at the same time toward the same person, called *ambivalence,* is illustrated in this short suicide note:

Dear Betty:
I hate you.
Love,
George

Shame and Disgrace

Some suicides seem to be related particularly to a sense of shame, "loss of face," disgrace or a sense of dereliction of duty. Prideful people especially seem vulnerable to these emotions. An example is the suicide of Dr. Paul Kammerer, an eminent Viennese biologist. His experiments with Alytes, the midwife toad (called that because the male toad wraps the fertilized eggs around his legs and carries them until they are hatched), attempted to prove the inheritance of certain acquired characteristics, specifically friction (or nuptial) pads on the front paws of the male toad, which helped him hold the female during mating. He had done fifteen years of very careful work, breeding and observing these toads, when it was discovered that injections of India ink had been made into the paws of the demonstration specimens, thus producing false results. Although it is not known whether he, or a laboratory assistant attempting to be helpful, did the forging, Kammerer was a ruined man.

In the woods near Vienna, in 1926, six weeks after he was accused, Kammerer shot himself through the head. Here is a translation of the suicide note found beside his body:

Letter to whosoever finds it:

Dr. Paul Kammerer begs not to be brought to his home so that his family might be spared the sight. It would be the simplest and cheapest way to use the body in a dissecting laboratory of a university. This would also be most agreeable to me since, in this way, I would render science at least a small service. Perhaps my esteemed colleagues will discover in my brain a trace of the qualities they found absent in the expressions of my intellectual activities while I was alive. Whatever happens to the corpse—burial, cremation or dissection—its owner belonged to no religious denomination and wishes to be spared any kind of religious ceremony which would probably be refused to him in any event. This is not animosity against any individual priest who is as human as the rest of us and often a good and noble person.[4]

There are several interesting details in this lugubrious document. The sense of shame, repentance and restitution are evident. His attitude toward himself as already a corpse is striking, but his inability to see himself as dead—Freud had written that no one can truly imagine his own death, but always remained a spectator—is seen in the contradiction that he does not care what happens to the corpse, but that he (the living man? the corpse? and if the corpse, what difference does it make?) wishes to be spared a religious ceremony. And there is a sense of counteraction: he rejects others before they reject him, as in his phrase ". . . which would probably be refused to him in any event."

And what is not in the note: statements of affection and wishes for forgiveness from his family, warmth, love. The note is largely a set of instructions: to the person who finds his body, to the pathologist who dissects his brain and to the priest who may or may not be good enough to conduct a tender ceremony. Finally, one can also infer that on an unconscious level, he views himself as a kind of priest of science who is as human as anyone and is really a good and noble person.

It seems to make most sense to view Kammerer's suicidal act

as an overwhelming concatenation, in a disturbed individual, of several emotional surges in addition to the overarching shame: anxiety, anger, depression, hopelessness, guilt, rejection; in other words, heightened general perturbation. All suicidal deaths are complicated events, but Kammerer's suicide seems more complex and more mysterious than most.

FEAR—SPECIFICALLY OF RECURRING INSANITY

Occasionally we find a suicide note that is rational in its irrationality, reflecting an act that we regret but nonetheless can understand. Virginia Woolf drowned herself in a small river, the Ouse, near her home in Sussex, England. She was a gifted woman, a literary celebrity, author of several novels in her special style emphasizing the flow of consciousness. She was also an editor, the founder, with her husband, of the Hogarth Press (which, among other famous books, printed Freud's works in English) and a key member of the so-called Bloomsbury group —a veritable who's who of creative individuals all concerned with the search for things good, true and beautiful.

In short, she was the hub of a radiant literary-philosophic wheel. But with all this, she still suffered—whether from genes or psychodynamics one cannot tell—crippling periods of mental incapacitation. In anyone, especially in a mature intellect, one of the most awesome fears is the niggling threat of losing one's hold on reality, of losing one's mind or going crazy. In 1941, these symptoms or presentiments began to reappear in Virginia Woolf. What they foreboded was simply too much for her to contemplate enduring, for herself and others. Here is her suicide note, addressed to her husband of almost thirty years:

> Dearest,
>
> I feel certain I am going mad again. I feel we can't go through another of those terrible times. And I shan't recover this time.

> I begin to hear voices, and I can't concentrate. So I am doing what seems the best thing to do. You have been in every way all that anyone could be. I don't think two people could have been happier till this terrible disease came. I can't fight any longer. I know that I am spoiling your life, that without me you could work. And I know you will. You see I can't even write this properly. I can't read. What I want to say is that I owe all the happiness of my life to you. You have been entirely patient with me and incredibly good. I want to say that—everybody knows it. If anybody could have saved me it would have been you. Everything has gone from me but the certainty of your goodness. I can't go on spoiling your life any longer.
>
> I don't think two people could have been happier than we have been.[5]

That note is both fearful and tender. She cannot bring herself to live through another period of psychosis, and more than that, she does not wish to burden her dear husband. The note, beginning with the reason for her desperate act, is then filled with feelings of hopelessness, concern, gratitude and love. The negative emotions are sparked by the desperation relating to her fears of her imminent madness. A significant part of that kind of malady is the inability to share one's secret terror—itself a symptom of the disturbed state of mind—with those who might have been the rescuers.

Traumatic Rejection and Self-Abnegation

The sense of total rejection, in a personality that already deprecates itself, is often a root cause of self-destruction. The cast of characters in the following tragedy is as complicated as it is well known. Fanny Imlay, later Fanny Imlay Godwin, had a star-crossed life seemingly from the moment she was conceived. Her genealogy is a bit complicated but bears careful tracing. She was born in 1794, the illegitimate daughter of Mary

Wollstonecraft, who was a famous feminist—the author of *The Rights of Women*—and of an American Revolutionary War captain named Imlay. Her mother then married William Godwin, a famous pamphleteer and political philosopher and novelist (he wrote *Caleb Williams*), and died a few days after having given birth to her half-sister, Mary Wollstonecraft Godwin (later the author of *Frankenstein*), who became the second wife of the poet Percy Bysshe Shelley. Thus Fanny was Shelley's half-sister-in-law—and in love with him. All her short life she was the odd one: illegitimate, half orphaned, excluded from the excitement of her half-sister's life, unnoticed or rejected by the beautiful Shelley, unemployed because of her famous but unsavory relatives, and living with the legacy of her own mother's suicide attempt when she was a young woman. In 1816, at age twenty-two, Fanny Godwin poisoned herself in an inn at an English seaside resort. This is her suicide note:

> I have long determined that the best thing I could do was to put an end to the existence of a being whose birth was unfortunate and whose life has only been a series of pains to those persons who have hurt their health in endeavoring to promote her welfare. Perhaps to hear of my death may give you pain, but you will soon have the blessing of forgetting that such a creature ever existed.[6]

The key words in this painful note are "being" and "creature." She is not a woman or a person or a human; she is just a biological thing that never should have been born. This is a note filled with nothingness; an overpowering sense of void and worthlessness. And to her mind, without love to fill that void, she might as well be dead.

In 1817, the year after Fanny's suicide, Shelley wrote a poem entitled "On Fanny Godwin."

> Her voice did quiver as we parted,
> Yet knew I not the heart was broken
> From which it came, and I departed

Heeding not the words then spoken.
Misery—O Misery,
This world is all too wide for thee.

"CREDO" SUICIDE NOTES

Some few suicide notes are written as creeds. They are essays about suicide itself, specifically about a man's moral and legal right to take his own life if he so chooses. The most famous piece of "credo" suicidal writing is not contained in a suicide note but in the essay "On Suicide" by the eighteenth-century Scottish philosopher David Hume. So controversial was it considered that it was not published until a year after his death.

In his essay, Hume—who died a natural death (apparently of cancer) at age sixty-five—sought to decriminalize suicide. In current terms, he might say that where the victim is oneself, it is an act within a consenting adult, and thus there is, in either the legal or the moral sense, no victim. Hume asserted that suicide is no crime; that there is no culprit; and, certainly, there is no sin.

Elton Hammond was an English eccentric who committed suicide at age thirty-three in 1819. Hammond was on the fringe of the literary life of eighteenth-century England.[7] He was somewhat peculiar, perhaps even insane. (He once announced to his sister that he was going to be greater than Jesus Christ.) But the main point here is not Hammond's mental health, but the clear way in which, in his suicide note, he stated a man's right to ownership of himself. It is an anti-clerical, anti-authoritarian credo.

It is likely that a man like Hammond would have known of Hume's essay. The similarities in thought and language between the two documents strongly suggest this possibility. But Hammond goes Hume one better; he is not only writing about his beliefs about suicide, he is putting his life where his mind is.

Here is his suicide note.

TO THE CORONER AND THE GENTLEMEN WHO WILL SIT ON MY BODY

Norwood, 31st Decr. 1819.

Gentlemen,

To the charge of self-murder I plead not guilty. For there is no guilt in what I have done. Self-murder is a contradiction in terms. If the King who retires from his throne is guilty of high treason; if the man who takes money out of his own coffers and spends it is a thief; if he who burns his own hayrick is guilty of arson; or he who scourges himself of assault and battery, then he who throws up his own life may be guilty of murder,—if not, not.

If anything is a man's own, it is surely his life. Far, however, be it from me to say that a man may do as he pleases with his own. Of all that he has he is a steward. Kingdoms, money, harvests, are held in trust, and so, but I think less strictly, is life itself. Life is rather the stewardship than the talent. The King who resigns his crown to one less fit to rule is guilty, though not of high treason; . . . the suicide who could have performed the duties of his station is perhaps guilty, though not of murder, not of felony. They are all guilty of neglect of duty, and all, except the suicide, of breach of trust. But I cannot perform the duties of my station. He who wastes his life in idleness is guilty of a breach of trust; he who puts an end to it resigns his trust,—a trust that was forced upon him, —a trust which I never accepted, and probably never would have accepted. Is this felony? I smile at the ridiculous supposition. How we came by the foolish law which considers suicide as felony I don't know; I find no warrant for it in Philosophy or Scripture.

I would rather be thrown naked into a hole in the road than that you should act against your consciences. But if you wish to acquit me, I cannot see your calling my death accidental, or the effect of insanity, would be less criminal than a jury's finding a £10 Bank-of-England note worth thirty-nine shillings, or premeditated slaying in a duel simple manslaughter, both of which have been done. But should you think this is too bold a

> course, is it less bold to find me guilty of *felo de se* when I am not guilty at all, as there is no guilt in what I have done? I disdain to take advantage of my situation as culprit to mislead your understandings, but if you, in your consciences, think premeditated suicide no felony, will you, upon your oaths, convict me of felony? Let me suggest the following verdict, as combining liberal truth with justice:—"Died by his own hand, but not feloniously." If I have offended God, it is for God, not you, to enquire. . . . I am free to-day, and avail myself of my liberty. I cannot be a good man, and prefer death to being a bad one—as bad as I have been and as others are.
>
> I take my leave of you and of my country condemning you all, yet with true honest love. . . . God bless you all!
>
> Elton

As a footnote to this suicide document, it is sad to relate that the coroner's jury did not accede to Hammond's request; they rendered a verdict of suicide by virtue of insanity—exactly what Hammond did not wish. (But this was done, in part, because Hammond's friend Henry Crabb Robinson did not turn over Hammond's letter to the jury, hoping, perhaps, to save his reputation.)

II

We have raised the question: What can we learn from suicide notes? Obviously, they often contain a great deal of interesting descriptive material, particularly of emotional states. But are they the full and explicating documents that would satisfactorily "explain" a suicide? The fact that a dozen and a half research studies by a score of qualified investigators over the past twenty years have *not* produced the new, important breakthroughs of information that one could legitimately expect from that amount of effort raises questions about their usefulness.

Overall, one might say that suicide notes are relatively barren compared with what we had hoped to find in them.[8] It seems as though we tend to confuse the drama of the suicidal situation with our own expectations that there be some dramatic psychodynamic insights in the communications written during the moments of that drama. But the fact remains that memorable (authenticated) words uttered *during* battle or *on* one's deathbed are rare. It seems to be true also of suicide notes. Understandably, however, we continue to hope that even an ordinary individual, standing on the brink of what man has always conceptualized as life's greatest adventure and mystery, ought to have some special message for the rest of us. Western civilization has for centuries romanticized death; we tend to read with special reverence and awe *any* words, however banal, that are part of a death-oriented document.

Perhaps suicide notes, by themselves, cannot be what we wanted them to be—for the plain and simple reason that they are written by a person whose mind (by virtue of being suicidal) is usually tunneled, overfocused, constricted and narrowed on a single goal.

A tragically precise and insightful description of tunneling and constriction is contained in the verbalization (reported in Chapter 2) of the young woman who jumped from a balcony.

> . . . I went into a terrible state. . . . I was so desperate . . . That's the *only* way to get away from it. The *only* way to lose consciousness. . . . everything just got very dark all of a sudden, and *all* I could see was this balcony. Everything around it just *blacked out.* It was just like a *circle.* That was *all* I could see, just the balcony . . . and I went over it. . . . [Italics added.]

As we read these chilling words we can practically visualize the constriction of her mind's focus, almost as the diaphragm of a fine camera closes down to its essential linear circle. And while this is happening, the mind's lens is adjusting to sharpen the focus on but a single objective. The objective is escape, specifically escape from intolerable emotion. It is at that precise moment of maximum constriction and focus that the picture is snapped; it is at that same moment when, as it were, the mind snaps and the act occurs.

Several suicidologists and literary writers have commented on the role of constriction in suicide. Margarethe von Andics[9] wrote a book about suicide (one hundred suicide attempts in Vienna in the 1940s) in which she emphasized the narrowing of the scope of consciousness that was characteristic of the suicidal state; Erwin Ringel, also of Vienna, has written extensively, since 1958, of what he calls the presuicidal syndrome, placing great emphasis on constriction.[10]

The contemporary English poet, novelist and critic A. Alvarez, who wrote an excellent book on suicide, *The Savage God,* has described what he calls "the closed world of suicide" in the following way:

> Once a man decides to take his own life he enters a shut-off, impregnable but wholly convincing world . . . where every detail fits and every incident reinforces his decision. . . . Each of these deaths has its own inner logic and unrepeatable despair. . . . [Suicide is] a terrible but utterly natural reaction to the strained, narrow, unnatural necessities we sometimes create for ourselves.[11]

Boris Pasternak, the famous author, writing of the suicide of several young Russian poets, has stated:

> A man who decides to commit suicide puts a full stop to his being, he turns his back on his past, he declares himself bankrupt and his memories to be unreal. They can no longer help or save him, he has put himself beyond their reach. The continuity of his inner life is broken, and his personality is at an end. And perhaps what finally makes him kill himself is not the firmness of his resolve but the unbearable quality of this anguish which belongs

> to no one, of this suffering in the absence of the sufferer, of this waiting which is empty because life is stopped and can no longer feel it.[12]

Because this sense of constriction exists in the suicidal person, is it any wonder that suicide notes, written at the very moment when an individual has lost touch with his own past, are taken up with minutiae and are in other ways relatively arid and psychologically barren?

Thus we see the relative barrenness of many—but not all—suicide notes can be psychologically explained. In order for a person to kill himself, he has to be in a special state of mind, a state of relatively fixed purposes (not to deny an ever-present ambivalence) and of relative constriction of the mind. It is a psychological state that, while it permits (indeed, facilitates) suicide, obviously militates against good insight or good communication. In other words, that special state of mind necessary to perform the suicidal deed is one which is essentially incompatible with an insightful recitation of what was going on in one's mind that led to the act itself. Suicide notes often seem like parodies of the postcards sent home from the Grand Canyon, the catacombs or the pyramids—essentially *pro forma,* not at all reflecting the grandeur of the scene being described or the depth of human emotions that one might expect to be engendered by the situation.

To state the case strongly: In order to commit suicide, one cannot write a meaningful suicide note; conversely, if one could write a meaningful note, one would not have to commit suicide. Or to put it in another way: In almost every instance, one has to be relatively intoxicated or drugged (by one's overpowering emotions and constricted logic and perception) in order to commit suicide, and it is well nigh impossible to write a psychologically meaningful document when one is in this disordered state.

Suicide notes, *by themselves,* may not tell us everything we want to know. Life is like a long letter and the suicide note is merely a postscript to it and cannot, by itself, be expected to carry the burden of substituting for the total document.

III

There is a vital reciprocity between suicide notes and the lives of which they are a part. This statement—my current position—is the synthesis of my two previous attitudes: the thesis that suicide notes by themselves are uniformly bountiful; and the antithesis that suicide notes have to be constricted and pedestrian documents. Suicide notes definitely can have a great deal of meaning (and give a great deal of information) when they are put in the context of the life history of the individual who both wrote the note and committed the act. In this situation—where we have *both* the suicide note and a *detailed* life history—then the note will illuminate aspects of the life history, and conversely, the life history can make many key words and ideas of the suicide note come alive and take on special meanings that would otherwise have remained hidden or lost. It is close to the art of biography.

Here are five suicide notes written by one woman (who committed suicide by barbiturate overdose) and many details of her life, to which these notes were but the final words.

In this case—Natalie, who killed herself at age forty—there were, in addition to her suicide notes, literally hundreds of separate personal documents and other records. They included the following: Early school records, teachers' notes to her parents, school physicians' reports, school evaluations, college records, several psychological tests, numerous questionnaires which she had completed, dozens of her letters and miscellaneous personal documents by the score. In all, there were over one hundred separate documents, including her suicide notes. (It took me many months to find them.)

We begin at the tragic end, with excerpts from the police report of her death:

On arrival, went through house into bathroom where victim was observed lying on the floor, head resting on a pillow, toward the west, feet pointed toward the east. Victim was dressed in a green bathrobe; was cold to the touch, rigor mortis having started to set in. On the pillow it was noted there was a stain, caused by a purge from the victim's mouth. Photographs of the scene were taken.

There was one small brown bottle with the label bearing prescription number and "One capsule at bed time . . ." This bottle was empty. Also a small plastic container was received with the label inside the cover reading "One tablet 4 times daily, regularly . . ." This container was also empty.

Undersigned spoke to [name and address], who stated he was victim's father. He further said that approximately two weeks ago, victim told him that she was going to commit suicide. He said he talked her out of the notion at that time, and did not figure she would make any further attempt on her life. He further said victim had been in ill health since her divorce and had been treated by a psychiatrist, address unknown; also that the victim had filed a will which is currently in the possession of her attorney.

While at location, victim's husband, [name], who gave address same as victim's, employed at Eastern Steel Corp., arrived and stated he would take care of his two children, Betty, 15 years; and Nancy, 10 years.

The investigating officer reported finding five suicide notes. I have made a few changes in identifying details:

1. To her adult friend:

Rosalyn—Get Eastern Steel Co.—Tell them and they will find Bob right away. Papa is at his business. Betty is at the Smiths—Would you ask Helene to keep her until her Daddy comes—so she won't know until he comes for her. You have been so good —I love you—Please keep in touch with Betty—Natalie

2. To her eldest daughter:

Betty, go over to Rosalyn's right away—Get in touch with Papa.

3. To her ex-husband, from whom she was recently divorced:

Bob—I'm making all kinds of mistakes with our girls—They have to have a leader and everyday the job seems more enormous—You couldn't have been a better Daddy to Nancy and they do love you—Nancy misses you so and she doesn't know what's the matter—I know you've built a whole new life for yourself but make room for the girls and keep them with you—Take them where you go—It's only for just a few years—Betty is almost ready to stand on her own two feet—But Nancy needs you desperately. Nancy needs help—She really thinks you didn't love her—and she's got to be made to do her part for her own self respect—Nancy hasn't been hurt much yet—but ah! the future if they keep on the way I've been going lately—Barbara sounds warm and friendly and relaxed and I pray to God she will understand just a little and be good to my girls—They need two happy people—not a sick mixed-up mother—There will be a little money to help with the extras—It had better go that way than for more pills and more doctor bills—I wish to God it had been different but be happy—but please—stay by your girls—And just one thing—be kind to Papa [*his* father]—He's done everything he could to try to help me—He loves the girls dearly and it's right that they should see him often—Natalie

Bob—this afternoon Betty and Nancy had such a horrible fight it scares me. Do you suppose Gladys and Orville would take Betty for this school year? She should be away from Nancy for a little while—in a calm atmosphere.

4. To her ex-father-in-law:

Papa—no one could have been more kind or generous than you have been to me—I know you couldn't understand this—and forgive me—[The lawyer] has a copy of my will—Everything

> equal—the few personal things I have of value—the bracelet to Nancy and my wedding ring to Betty—But I would like Betty to have Nana's diamond—have them appraised and give Betty and Nancy each half the diamonds in the band. Please have somebody come in and clean—Have Bob take the girls away immediately—I don't want them to have to stay around—You're so good Papa dear—

5. To her two children:

> My dearest ones—You two have been the most wonderful things in my life—Try to forgive me for what I've done—Your father would be so much better for you. It will be harder for you for awhile—but so much easier in the long run—I'm getting you all mixed up—Respect and love are almost the same—Remember that—and the most important thing is to respect yourself—The only way you can do that is by doing your share and learning to stand on your own two feet—Betty, try to remember the happy times—and be good to Nancy. Promise me you will look after your sister's welfare—I love you very much—but I can't face what the future will bring.

A number of sad observations can be made about these suicide notes. The despairing writer of them seems so pushed, so weary, so harried, so beaten by life. She has capitulated. Not atypically, the notes—especially the first two—contain directions, words like "get," "ask," "tell," "go." The disposition of affection is curious: It can be seen in different forms of the salutation and the complimentary close. The only use of "dear" or "dearest" is with her children and her ex-father-in-law. Words of love are reserved only for her neighbor-friend and for her children. There is no note to either of her living parents, both of whom resided nearby.

Her note to her ex-husband is a painful *mea culpa.* She takes all blame and pleads to him—a man who drank quite a bit and was impossible for her to live with—to be good to their children. In an amazing turn-about, she asks that the new stepmother and her ex-husband provide a stable home for her girls.

Her life can be retraced from the available materials. The conditions of her birth were noted as "absolutely normal." She was breast fed until she was two months old. As an infant, she slept soundly.

At the age of five and a half she was given dancing lessons. There is a note that she was very enthusiastic and showed decided ability. When Natalie was six, her mother wrote to a friend that "Edgar Guest's poems are her great favorites." In that same letter, the mother wrote: "I have tried to use a lot of common sense and have answered every question to the best of my ability because she is an understanding child and will listen to reason. I have not had to stimulate a desire to learn because she always wanted to know everything her older playmates knew and she would try to learn voluntarily."

She had a brother, who was eight years older than she. Later she would say about him that "he could never make a living."

When Natalie was six years old, in the first grade, she was given an individual intelligence test. One item that she missed —although she scored extremely high overall, with an I.Q. of over 153, which put her in the extremely superior category— was this one: "Yesterday the police found the body of a girl cut into 18 pieces. They believed that she killed herself. What is foolish about that?" Her nonprophetic answer was "She wouldn't kill herself." The psychologist noted, however, her general alertness and her extremely logical mind.

A very important event occurred in Natalie's life when she was seven: her father deserted her mother. Later in her life, she noted, with obvious sadness, that *"My father never came to see me except once."*

The records of her childhood medical examinations are interesting. One, written by a school physician when she was eight, states that she was "somewhat nervous, bordering on irritability," and that she had some loss of hearing in her right ear. A school record when she was eleven notes that her last name had been changed to reflect the fact that her mother had divorced and remarried. The teacher's report states that she was a "youngster with an understanding and reasoning little mind that at times surprises her family" and that "her courtesy and tact are remarkable."

At age twelve there are several items of interest. She suffered from numerous headaches and had glasses prescribed. She reported that she still had disturbing eye strain even with glasses. She experienced her menarche; she was a straight A student (in the seventh grade) and indicated that she wanted to go to college and that she would also like to be a dancer. Her hearing loss had increased and she was somewhat sensitive about it; she would not admit this difficulty to any of her teachers. Her main teacher reported that although she was extremely bright, she "shrinks from opportunities for leadership." At about this time, she wrote a letter in which she indicated that her new stepfather was devoted and kind to her and her brother. Perhaps this helps to explain her unusual attitude to her girls' new stepmother (in the note to her ex-husband).

She finished high school and went on to college for three years but did not graduate. At college she developed a close, lasting student-teacher relationship with a distinguished professor; she wrote detailed letters to him for years. At the age of twenty-five, having, in her own words, been "an unsuccessful secretary," her "ultimate goal" was to "be a successful homemaker." She married and in the two following years lived in five different cities. Understandably, she wrote that "it is hard to develop interests in any one place." She became pregnant almost immediately after getting married.

There is a gap in the records for five years. At age thirty she had two children and reports a "great tendency to worry and extreme nervousness." Her husband was drinking rather heavily. There was a dramatic change in her own physical and psychological state. She reported that she was "too tired even to wash the windows." She also reported a sharp pain in her side, which her doctor told her was due to "neurotic tendencies."

She wrote that she was "chronically worn out and tired and very unhappy in the marriage."

There is a painful letter to her favorite college professor, written when she was about thirty-five:

> . . . Until I was 25 I didn't know there were such things as problems in this world, but since then with the exception of my two lovely children and my perfect relationship with my mother, I've had just one struggle after another, made one blunder after another. My husband and I bicker constantly. I've wanted to divorce him a thousand times and still I know that is not the solution. We were both raised in broken homes and we both love our children too much. He comes home drunk at night far too often. He can't afford it. He refuses to look at the bills and says "Why haven't you saved money?" I have no one to talk to. I feel like I'm cornered. . . . My mother's youngest brother and my nearest neighbor both committed suicide in one month [about a year before].

In this same communication, writing about her misfortunes in general, she said this about her father: "I adored my father from afar. Our occasional meetings were unsatisfactory. My father is a very brilliant man—however *he has little use for me* —He lives 20 minutes away but has been in our home only once for a few minutes in the past two years." Those lines strike a key theme in her broken life. She said that she was reading Menninger's *Man Against Himself*—a book about suicide.

In another letter she wrote of her children:

> Our little ones are nice, but the eldest still bites her fingernails and fights constantly with her younger sister. She is the result of my selfishness. . . . Well, I've poured out my heart and I'm a little ashamed. In my heart I've never doubted that I can be a happy, relaxed, useful human being, but it's taking such a long time to get there.

Four years later, when Natalie was thirty-nine, she separated from her husband, because—from another letter—of "his violent temper, his selfishness and his drinking." Nine months later she was divorced. Four months after the divorce was final (and he had already remarried), she was dead of suicide.

What deep psychological strains motivate such an act? When we read about her life, especially the subtleties of interaction with her father, we can see the malignant beginnings of her self-abnegating attitudes. At the end, she is so frantic that she will give anything, make any votive offering, including her life, to achieve the feeling of childhood love.

In her suicide she reenacted her own earlier life drama—the yearning for her parents to be together—and in this misdirected symbolic sacrifice, instead of giving her children a (seemingly) united home, she, in the most traumatic way possible, deprived them of their own mother. Her aspirations—to be her father's favorite, to be accepted and not abandoned, to care for and not reject her own children (as she had been rejected and not cared for), to be symbolically reunited with her father in a happy home, to sacrifice herself so that some of the problems of her children might be solved—were no better realized in her death than they were in her life.

Natalie's suicide note to her children is filled with contradictions and inconsistencies. (We remember that when she was tested as a child, the psychologist called her extremely logical.) In the suicide note, the implicit logical arguments flow back and forth, between assertion and counterassertion, never with any resolution. Here are some examples: She says, in effect, you will stay with your father, you should love your father, I know that you cannot love your father but at least you must respect him. She then almost free-associates to the word "respect" and argues, rather lamely, that love and respect are almost the same anyway, and in case that argument is not persuasive (which it is not), then one should, at least, respect one's self. The logic wanders.

Another sad example: She says to her children, You must stand on your own two feet, but she also implies that the point of her removing herself from their lives is so that they can be reunited with their father—as, probably, she unconsciously yearns to be reunited with her father.

To tell one's children in a suicide note to remember the happy times certainly has some contradictory element in it, on the very face of it. I love you so much, she says, but the end result of her actions is to make them orphans. She adds, I can't face what the future will bring, but she then takes her life largely because of the haunting, inescapable past. And finally, there is her statement, "I'm getting you all mixed up," which obviously betokens the confusion not in their minds but in her own.

The connections between suicide notes and other aspects of a life seem inescapable with Natalie. The first has to do with Natalie's passivity, her fear of aggression and her fear of violence. In her suicide note she says that the children have to have a leader; when she was twelve, her teacher reported that she shrank from opportunities for leadership. It would appear that all her life she wanted love given to her; in her childhood, and as a wife and mother, she was afraid to stand up for her legitimate rights. She feared and hated quarreling. In the note she said, about the girls, that one afternoon they had "such a horrible fight it scared me." Indeed it must have—adding to her feelings of helplessness and hopelessness, feelings that are part of the suicidal scene.

Another connecting thread can be found between the poignant item contained in the letter she wrote around age thirty-five in which she says, "I adored my father from afar. . . . however *he has little use for me,*" and all the pleading for her children in her suicide notes. In her note to her friend she says: "Please keep in touch with Betty"; and to her ex-husband: "Nancy misses you so . . . [and] needs you desperately . . . [and] really thinks you didn't love her . . . be good to my girls." If one substitutes her name for her girls', one can read the notes as though they were addressed to her own father, whom she could not bring herself—out of a mixture of hostility, rejection and yearning—to contact. At the end, her love is expressed to her ex-father-in-law: "You're so good Papa dear." Finally, in a state of psychological bankruptcy, she tells her children: "Your father would be so much better for you." She is depleted, tired, exhausted, burned out. "I can't face what the future would bring," she says. For her, it would be more of the same. The notes *and* the life both tell us so.

It should now be evident that suicide notes, written, as they are, as part of the life that they reflect, can have a great deal of meaning (and give us a great deal of scientific and clinical information) when they are examined in light of the details of the full life history of which they are the penultimate act. By putting a suicide note within the context of the life history of the individual (who both wrote the note and committed the act), one can find that many words, ideas, emotional proclivities, styles of reaction, modes of thinking, etc., that characterized that life are reflected in the specific details of the suicide note. And conversely, many words, phrases, ideas, passions, emphases, etc., contained in the suicide note are extensions of those very same threads that had previously characterized the life. Living or dying, a particular individual has a certain consistency, a certain "unity thema," a certain "trademark," which he or she will show in work style, in play style and in life style, whether celebrating life in a poem of love or contemplating death in a note of suicide.

There is a bizarre but fascinating and incredibly inventive novel, *The Dwarf,* by the contemporary Swedish author Pär Lagerkvist—winner of the 1951 Nobel Prize in literature—about an aberrant and evil dwarf (in a medieval Italian prince's court), which, by sheer coincidence, contains uncanny and tragic parallels to an actual contemporary case that I know. Indeed, the gruesome similarities (in what a sadistic monster can do to a sensitive child) between that honored work of fiction and the actual case are so striking that I have decided to present the two in tandem. My purpose is not to focus on the monsters, but rather on their victims. First, let us read some passages from the novel. It begins:[13]

> I am twenty-six inches tall, shapely and well proportioned, my head perhaps a trifle too large. My hair is not black like the others', but reddish, very stiff and thick, drawn back from the temples and the broad but not especially lofty brow. My face is beardless, but otherwise just like that of other men. My eyebrows meet. My bodily strength is considerable, particularly if I am annoyed. When the wrestling match was arranged between Jehoshaphat and myself I forced him onto his back after twenty minutes and strangled him. Since then I have been the only dwarf at this court.

One of the several subplots in *The Dwarf* concerns the prince's young daughter, Angelica. Here is an excerpt:

> There is a great difference between dwarfs and children. Because they are about the same size, people think that they are alike, and that they suit each other; but they do not. Dwarfs are set to play with children, forced to do so. It is nothing less than torture to use us dwarfs like that. But human beings know nothing about us.
>
> My masters have never forced me to play with Angelica, but she herself has done so. That infant, whom some people think so wonderful with her round blue eyes and her little pursed mouth, has tormented me almost more than anyone else at court.
>
> We visit her dolls which have to be fed and dressed, the rose garden where we have to play with the kitten. . . . She can sit and play with her kitten for ages and expect me to join in. She believes that I too am a child with a child's delight in everything. I! I delight in nothing.

And then the dwarf's revenge on the child:

> Once I crept into her room as she lay sleeping with her detestable kitten beside her in bed and cut off its head with my dagger. Then I threw it into the dungheap beneath the castle window. She was inconsolable when she saw that it was gone, and when everybody said that of course it must be dead, she sickened with an unknown fever and was ill for a long time, so that I, thank goodness, did not have to see her.

And finally, the dwarf's ultimate revenge on Angelica when she has grown up to be a young woman: He informs the prince, his master, that Angelica is being visited by a lover, who is, of all people, the scion of the prince's hated rival family. The prince is furious.

> "Impossible!" he maintained. "Nobody can come into the town over the river, between the fortresses on both banks where archers keep watch night and day. It is absolutely unthinkable!" . . .
>
> "Yes, it is unthinkable," I admitted . . . but think if the criminal had already slipped away! Or if both had fled! The horrible suspicion sent me flying over the courtyard as fast as my legs could carry me, and up the stairs to Angelica's door.
>
> I put my ear against it. No sound within! Had they fled? I slipped inside and immediately recovered my composure. To my joy I saw them sleeping side by side in her bed, by the light of a little oil lamp that they had forgotten to extinguish.
>
> Now I heard the Prince and his men on the stairs, and presently he came in followed by two sentinels. Livid with wrath he snatched the sword from one of the sentinels and with a single blow severed Giovanni's head from his body. Angelica woke up and stared with wild dilated eyes as they dragged her gory lover from her couch and flung him on to the muckheap outside the window. Then she fell back in a swoon and did not recover consciousness as long as we remained in the room.

In the town there is a plague; Angelica suffers a rather peculiar and different malady:

> Angelica cannot be sick of this plague. Her malady is the same as that which she once had as a child. I do not quite remember when, nor the exact circumstances. She has always been rather sickly, for reasons which could not possibly affect anybody else's health. Ah, now I remember. It was when I cut off her kitten's head.

Finally, Angelica is driven to despair:

> Angelica has drowned herself in the river. She must have done it yesterday evening or last night, for nobody saw her. She left a letter behind which leaves no doubt that she killed herself in that manner. Throughout the day they have been searching for her body, all the length of the river where it flows through the beleaguered city, but in vain. Like Giovanni's it must have been carried away by the tides.
>
> There is a great to-do at the court. Everybody is upset and cannot realize that she is dead. I see nothing extraordinary about the letter, and it changes nothing—certainly not the crime which was committed and which everybody condemned unanimously. It contains nothing new.
>
> I had to hear it again and again until I know it almost by heart. It runs something like this:
>
>> I do not want to stay with you any longer. You have been so kind to me, but I do not understand you. I do not understand how you could take my beloved away from me, my dear one who came so far from another country to tell me that there was a thing called love.
>>
>> As soon as I met him, I knew why life had been so strangely difficult up to then.
>>
>> Now I do not want to stay here, where he is not, but I shall follow him. I shall just lay myself down to rest on the river, and God will take me where I am to go.
>>
>> You must not believe that I have taken my life, for I have only done as I was told. And I am not dead. I have gone to be joined forever to my beloved.
>>
>> I forgive you with all my heart.
>>
>> Angelica.

> The Princess is convinced that she is the cause of Angelica's death. This is the first time I have ever known her to take any interest in her child. She scourges herself more than ever to efface this sin, eats nothing at all, and prays to the Crucified One for forgiveness.
>
> The Crucified One does not answer.

Now let us turn to a real-life tragedy: the suicide of a twenty-three-year-old woman. I shall call her Dolores. This occurred in the 1970s, in a large city in the United States, in a motel room. She had brought with her a copy of Alvarez's *The Savage God* (in which he discusses the suicide of the poet Sylvia Plath). She registered under the name "Marilyn Plath." She hanged herself from the shower. She left this suicide note:

> Forgive me. It was too late for me to be repaired. No one is to blame. I love you all. I want to be buried here. I am a broken doll. I have been to too many doll hospitals. They couldn't repair me. So dear doctor and Gregor, you were working against the impossible. How can a doll that has been through a mangler be repaired? I love you all for your great loving effort. Remember me with happiness for now I shall have no more pain.

Some few weeks before that eventful day, she had spontaneously written another personal document, a sort of essay of anguish, which she had entitled "What Is Depression?" Here it is, verbatim:

> Depression is feeling revulsion from one's mother as a child. Depression is hoping to be the greatest love in someone's life and realizing it will never be so. Depression is knowing that although Maria, my nana as a child, loved me she went along all the way with the very strong mistress of the house, my charming mother, who constantly punished me for small reasons and instructed my nana to do the same. Depression is knowing that my family loved me but was told how bad I was, so love was limited. Depression is fear of having wanted to reach out to my mother and getting rejection in return. Depression is caring but beginning to stop

reaching out. Depression is being a showpiece, the best dressed little girl. Who could say she hadn't the perfect mother? She dressed you so well—you have the nicest clothes—what a lucky girl you are to have such a wonderful mother. Depression is being noticed by my mother in public and ignored by her in private. Depression is knowing that I am being blackmailed by a little brother who knows he is the chosen one and having to do as he says. Depression is knowing that father loved me but never stood up for me—my mother was the master of the house. Depression is hearing over and over the story of my birth. The disappointment experienced by my mother of having had a girl. Depression is not really knowing if I was such an awful child—not being certain I couldn't have been such a revulsion without doing some great wrong. Depression is not remembering the wrong things. My father slept with a gun under his pillow—my mother told me I had access to it one day—that I pointed it at my mother and that it was taken away. I was about 3 and don't remember. *Depression was the killing of my dog and the murder of my doll by my brother.* [Italics added.] Depression is the development of hate, knowing that whatever I do I won't be loved. Depression was the encouragement of my parents telling my teacher to constantly punish me if I did anything incorrectly. Depression was being caned at school and beaten at home for having had to be caned at school. Depression is doing everything to be loved—but my mother saw to it that no one was going to love me. Depression is seeing love happening and suddenly disappearing. Depression is hearing that my brother makes my family so happy and I am a constant crown of thorns. Depression is my brother convincing me that if I put sugar in my hands bees will make honey for me—Depression is being stung and having my mother laugh heartily for my brother's cleverness and my stupidity. Depression is hearing this hilarious story repeated over and over. Depression is the fright of being stung by a bee for the first time and wanting to be held and comforted and receiving laughter at my stupidity. Depression is knowing in life there is no real love—that love will die or the person will leave me.

There is so much more but I don't want to think anymore right

> now—but I hate her and all the people who couldn't love me just for me. They would just begin to love me and then they would meet her and the love for me would stop almost immediately. I am never going to let her take anyone from me again. I will do anything however wrong to prevent this—however drastic. I will stop at nothing.

This remarkable psychological document is a painfully shrill cry of hate and hurt. It is the wail of the psychologically rejected child; the lament of the unfavorite sibling.

Dolores was born in a major city in South America. Her parents were well-to-do and sent her to a fancy school—where she was beaten. After she finished high school in her native country, she came to the United States, attended a large university and had a lover, named Gregor. He was a tender man and extremely solicitous of Dolores's feelings. For some months before she died she was in psychotherapy. The following is a summary of some of her early memories as related to me by her therapist:

> When she was born, in the hospital, her mother refused to look at her because she was not a boy. Dolores knew this well because her mother reminded her of it again and again, but also because she was also told this by the nurse when she was old enough to remember. Her mother did not look at her until she brought her home and then she was taken care of by this nana. Dolores has distinct memories back to about the age of four. Those crucial memories were somewhere between four and six. The critical memory is that she had a doll. It was an ordinary doll, nothing very special about it, but she absolutely adored it. One day she couldn't find this doll. They lived in a large house which had a walled-in garden and wooden pickets all the way around the garden, and she couldn't find her beloved doll and went out and there she saw, on top of one of those pickets, just the head of her doll impaled on the fence. The rest of it her impish brother had destroyed. [The brother verified that memory to the therapist.] But her feeling was that he had killed her doll and her dog and she said that over and over.

> There is another memory which goes back to that time. These memories were also verified by her brother. This other memory—which dates back to a very young age—is of her grandmother's house, which was apparently not too far away from their house. Across from her grandmother's house there was a cemetery. Dolores remembers going often to the cemetery when she was very despairing, having been punished by her mother. At the age of four or five she would go to the cemetery whenever there was a funeral and she would sit and watch the mourners and all the beautiful flowers and she would say to herself, Oh, I wish someone would love me enough to care. She remembers her feelings of rejection as early as that.*

The skeins of death were woven into her life almost from the beginning. Could it be that she was responding to her mother's unconscious (or even conscious) messages that things would be better if she, Dolores, were dead? A miserable childhood and the subtle parental cruelties of a lifetime can be a lethal potion.

When she was a young adult, her lover's concern and devotion could not pierce the impenetrable wall of Dolores's fixed feelings of being unlovable. In her distorted view of life, no one could give her enough love. Even her intense positive relationship with her psychotherapist was, not unexpectedly, contaminated with a fatal drop of deep childhood ambivalence.

The key imagery is that of the broken doll. The "broken doll" in the suicide note directly parallels the "murder of my doll" in the life history. In the same sense that the doll of her childhood was hopelessly destroyed and could never be repaired, she felt that neither could she—another broken doll that had been through life's mangler—be propped up enough to live.

Although there was no actual dwarf in her life, her mischievous little brother, encouraged by the mother, was the impish and sadistic figure in her childhood. Like the dwarf, he was a monster. There were also other symbolic monsters in her life

*Compare these lugubrious thoughts with the similar memories of the young woman who immolated herself, reported in Chapter 2.

(such as her unbearable feelings of rejection), which finally broke her delicate spirit.

In these two cases, then, we can begin to appreciate the reciprocal relationship between the suicide notes and the lives themselves.

Part Two

Enemies, Without and Within

4

Execution: Letters of Enforced Death

> These men are true madmen, and of the most dangerous sort, for their lunacy is not continuous but occasional evoked by some special object; it is probably secretive which is as much to say it is self-contained, so that when moreover, most active it is to the average mind not distinguishable from sanity, and for the reason above suggested that whatever its aims may be, and the aim is never declared the method and the outward proceeding are always perfectly rational.
>
> Now something such was Claggart, in whom was the mania of an evil nature, not engendered by vicious training or corrupting books or licentious living, but born with him and innate, in short "a depravity according to nature."
>
> Herman Melville, *Billy Budd*
> (Chapter XI)

When one is contemplating suicide, one is obviously on one's own and is likely to be in the grip of ambivalences (about love and hate, life and death) at their neurotic worst. It is thus little wonder that the documents of death under these circumstances —suicide notes—are sometimes filled with trivia and psychologically inconsequential thoughts and ideas, as well as with the negative side of the inner life: hostility, revenge, shame, guilt, fear, dependency, self-deprecation and so on. Rarely is the suicidal state the moment to be noble. Suicide is one's own doing and displays both the desperation and the neurotic elements that make the act seem "reasonable" when it is committed. The suicidal person is always in psychological pain, wishing to escape intolerable emotional distress.

The threat of being executed is psychologically entirely different from suicide. The menace comes from the *outside,* from a powerful "other," and the villains are real. In this circumstance there is little time to be neurotic; one has to marshal all one's inner forces against the palpably murderous enemy. Ambivalences are put aside; the mind is clear. If one is to write at all, the task is straightforward: It is to pen one last communiqué, unencumbered by trivia, to one's loved ones. Execution notes are, by and large, unusual psychological documents—unusual in their lucidity, their compassion for loved ones, and the expression of a sense of peace. To characterize these last notes or farewell letters, we need to reach back to old-fashioned phrases like "righteous indignation" and "the courage of one's own convictions."

In this situation of great duress, when one *knows* that one is going to be killed soon, the human personality tends to husband itself, gathering together all possible psychological energy. There is no time for petty emotion. One is beyond hope and thus—having been flung, alive (at least for a little while), over those dangerous rapids (of having been sentenced to death)—one can be beyond fears for oneself. In that quiet pond—just before the fatal catastrophic waterfall ahead—one can disengage oneself from the usual anxieties, aspirations and views of one's "ordinary" life, with its daily stresses and "unlimited time," and, for a fleeting moment, rise, unencumbered, to a state of being at true peace with oneself. Then it is possible, with the trappings of life's neurotic pressures fallen away, to write a last letter that is complete, rounded off, filled with genuine compassion for others and signed boldly. Thus these letters often have an unusual clarity, maturity and profundity.

People who are about to die think intensively about themselves. They think about being alive and about what the world will be like after they are dead. In a very understandable and psychologically legitimate way, they mourn themselves. This phenomenon—called self-mourning or auto-mourning—occurs not only with the threat of execution but also with the forebodings of a life-threatening disease like cancer or leukemia, and is dealt with in more detail in Chapter 5.

The following death document of auto-mourning is rather unusual. It is a poem, written by an Elizabethan courtier, filled with ironic juxtaposition, expressed in a highly controlled and stylized way. In the sixteenth century it was the fashion to write of life's greatest problems in poetic form.

Chidiock Tichborne was a young gentleman, a Roman Catholic, who became involved in a plot against the life of Queen Elizabeth. The plot was discovered, he was apprehended, taken to the Tower of London and sentenced to death. Here is "Tichborne's Elegy, Written in the Tower Before His Execution, 1586."[1] He was twenty-eight years old.

My prime of youth is but a frost of cares;
 My feast of joy is but a dish of pain;
My crop of corn is but a field of tares;
 And all my good is but vain hope of gain:
The day is past, and yet I saw no sun;
And now I live, and now my life is done.

My tale was heard, and yet it was not told;
 My fruit is fall'n, and yet my leaves are green;
My youth is spent, and yet I am not old;
 I saw the world, and yet I was not seen:
My thread is cut, and yet it is not spun;

And now I live, and now my life is done.

I sought my death, and found it in my womb;
  I looked for life, and saw it was a shade;
I trod the earth, and knew it was my tomb;
  And now I die, and now I was but made:
My glass is full, and now my glass is run;
And now I live, and now my life is done.

What moves us in that poem is the capacity of a human being —even a potential regicide—under the direst of conditions to funnel his feelings into an act of creative intellectual endeavor; to convert his emotions into a pensive philosophic thought; to impose discipline upon a racing heart.

If, as legend has it, Tichborne wrote this poem on the eve of his execution, then it is certainly one of the most remarkable death documents in the world, attesting to the power of the human spirit to give form to passion, to convert internal anarchy to poetry. When Tichborne was faced with the unchangeable, he mourned his own demise, accepted what was immutable and turned his sorrow into art.

Psychologically, a police state—and in its extreme form, a concentration camp—is a place where slavery is practiced. The master-slave relationship—whimsical and/or sadistic control, without accountability, over the welfare and the very life of another human being—often brings out the absolute worst in man. The opportunity, and with it the temptation, to be cruel (and to think of the other human being as less than a human being) is simply too beguiling. To enslave another person (through the power, say, of barbed wire, whips and weapons) debases the masters, reducing them to beasts.

Psychopathic genocide—icy planning of mass murder without a qualm of conscience—has never been seen on the scale in which it occurred in this century. In his searing work *The Twentieth Century Book of the Dead,* Gil Elliot documents the unspeakable arithmetic of the 110 million people—"a nation of the dead"—who have been murdered by organized state governments since 1900.[2] The villains have been certain segments among the Russians, Chinese, Turks, Poles, nationalistic or tribal Arab and African groups, and many others, including especially those archvillains the Nazis.

Understandably, very few documents that were written by the victims of the Nazi concentration camps have survived. Three fragmentary diaries are reproduced in a publication called *Amidst a Nightmare of Crime.*[3] The title was requested by one of the anonymous murdered writers. The booklet is published by the State Museum of Oświecim (Auschwitz). Here is how one of the manuscripts was found: "On October 17, 1962—about twenty years after—in the course of a search conducted in the vicinity of the ruins of crematorium III at Birkenau, a jar was found buried in the ground near the gas chamber. . . . a roll of papers was found in the jar, which proved to be a small notebook. . . . Altogether there were 65 leaves in the jar. The leaves in the notebook were covered with writing on both sides. . . . 40% of the text was illegible. The manuscript, except for one page in Polish, is written in Yiddish. . . ." It speaks for six million Jews. It tells of unimaginable barbarities and atrocities. Here is the very last entry of one diary:

> Today in crematorium III 600 boys were brought in the middle of a bright day 600 Jewish boys aged from 12 to 18, very thin; their feet were shod in worn out shoes or wooden clogs. The boys looked so handsome and were so well-built that even these rags did not mar their beauty. This happened in the latter part of October [1944]. They were brought by 25 SS men, heavily burdened with grenades. When they came to the square the SS men gave the order for them to undress in the square. The boys noticed the smoke belching from the chimney and at once guessed that they were being led to death. They began running hither and thither in the square in wild terror, tearing their hair, not knowing how to save themselves. Many burst into horrible

> tears; there resounded dreadful lamentation. An SS man beat the defenseless boys horribly to make them undress. His club broke even owing to that beating. So he brought another and continued the beating over the heads until violence became victorious. The boys undressed, instinctively afraid of death, naked and barefooted they herded together in order to avoid the blows and did not budge from the spot. One brave boy approached the SS man and begged him to spare his life, promising he would do even the hardest work. In reply he hit him several times over the head with a thick club. Many boys ran in a wild hurry. . . . Others scurried naked all over the big square in order to escape from death. The SS man called the Unterscharfuhrer [Corporal] with a rubber truncheon to his assistance. The young clear boyish voices resounded louder and louder with every minute, when at last they passed into bitter sobbing. This dreadful lamentation was heard from very far. We stood completely aghast as if paralyzed by this mournful weeping. With a smile of satisfaction, without a trace of compassion, looking like proud victors, the SS men stood and dealing terrible blows drove them into the bunker. The Unterscharfuhrer stood on the steps and should anyone run too slowly to meet death he would deal a murderous blow with the rubber truncheon. Some boys, in spite of everything, still continued to scurry hither and thither in the square, seeking salvation. The SS men followed them, beat and belabored them, until they had mastered the situation and at last drove them into the bunker. Their joy was indescribable. Did they not have any children ever?

Sardonically, one has to admit that in a certain evil way, the Nazis were even-handed, capable of treating their own citizens and soldiers with a callousness that most people usually reserve only for their worst enemies. An extensive example of the Nazis' ruthlessness with their own can be seen in the handling of the last letters of doomed soldiers to their loved ones.[4] In August 1942, the German Sixth Army invaded Russia up to the Volga River, opposite Stalingrad. By September, the Russians were beginning to counterattack; in November, a Russian tank army made a pincer movement around the 240,000 German troops. The Sixth Army was trapped and—under Hitler's direct command—was left there to perish. In January 1943, when food and ammunition (and time) were obviously running out, the German soldiers were told that there would be one last airplane flying out and that they might write one letter. But under an order issued by Hitler's headquarters, there was never any intention of delivering the mail. It was merely a device to ascertain the morale of the troops. In fact, the letters were so critical of the German Supreme Command that Goebbels had the results suppressed. Eventually the letters were found by the Allied forces.

The German Sixth Army was destroyed by the Russians on February 2, 1943. Most of the men died. Here are excerpts from two of those last letters:

> I shall never return. Break it to our parents gently. I am deeply shaken and doubt everything. I used to be strong and full of faith; now I am small and without faith. I will never know many of the things that happen here; but the little that I have taken part in is already so much that it chokes me. No one can tell me any longer that the men die with the words "Deutschland" or "Heil Hitler" on their lips. There is plenty of dying, no question of that; but the last word is "mother" or the name of someone dear.

> They told us this morning that we could write. Just one more I say, for I know definitely that this will be the last time. You know that I always wrote to two people, two women, to the "other one" and you. . . . Today, however, when fate gives me the choice of writing to one person only, my letter goes to you, who have been my wife for six years. The last letter of the man whom you loved is directed to you. So keep me alive in your memory as the man who recalled only at the very end that he is your husband and who asks your forgiveness; more, asks you to tell everyone you know, Carola included, that I found my way back to you at the moment which will take you away from me forever.

Here, from another source,[5] are some notes written in the same year by a twentieth-century Czechoslovakian journalist, Julius Fucik. He was arrested by the Gestapo on April 24, 1942, and executed on September 8, 1943, in Berlin. An unknown person somehow rescued the notes and letters he wrote during his incarceration.

> . . . Hopes drop away silently, gone limp like wilted leaves. Poetic souls when they see this sometimes fall prey to longing. Winter prepares man for its rigors as it prepares a tree. Believe me, this has taken nothing, absolutely nothing, from the joy that is in me and that heralds itself each day with some Beethoven theme or other. Man does not become smaller even when he becomes shorter by a head. And my ardent wish is that when all is over you will remember me not with sorrow, but with precisely that joy with which I always lived.

That letter was addressed to his parents just after he had heard that he was to be shot. He then wrote a note "To the Survivors," which contains a basic request that stands as the plea of all the victims:

> . . . I ask for one thing: you who will survive this era, *do not forget.* Forget neither the good men nor the evil. Gather together patiently the testimonies about those who have fallen.

His last written sentence was: "Mankind, I loved you. Be vigilant!"

Fucik's letter to his parents invokes an arboreal imagery of life as a tree, wilting, dying, that is often seen in letters written before executions. Here is another, written a year later by Nikolaus von Halen—lawyer, businessman, poet and anti-Nazi—a few minutes before he was executed by the Nazis in October 1944, at the age of thirty-nine. This brief letter, written with manacled hands, was addressed—as many last letters are—to his beloved mother:

> Now I have overcome the last little tremor that seizes the top of the tree before it falls. And with this I have attained the goal

of humanity. For we can and must endure consciously that which plants undergo without consciousness.

Adieu. They are coming to get me.

A thousand kisses.
Your son[6]

The archenemy of forests is fire. Here are some excerpts from the letter by a forty-year-old jurist and high-ranking official (before the Nazi regime), Peter, Count Yorck von Wartenburg, who was an outspoken anti-Nazi. He was executed in August 1944. He wrote to his mother and his wife. Here are the first and last paragraphs of his letter to his wife—which illustrate again the pride a person can take in his own victimization when he believes he is right.

> We have probably come to the end of the beautiful, rich life we have lived in common. For tomorrow the People's Court will sit in judgment on me and the others. I hear that the army has expelled us: they can take our garments, but not the spirit in which we acted. And in this spirit I feel myself in union with my forebears and my brothers and also with my comrades. . . . Though in appearance my death is an inglorious, even shameful one, I tread this last path erect and unbowed, and I hope only that you will not see this as arrogance and delusion. We meant to kindle the torch of life. And now a sea of fire engirds us—and what a fire![7]

Baron Alexis von Roenne was a colonel of the German Army. From the beginning of National Socialism, he regarded it and Hitler as a disaster for Germany. His own conscience prevented him from taking an active role in the preparation of the attempted coup on Hitler's life (on July 20, 1944, when a bomb was placed within a briefcase beneath the table at command headquarters), but his ties to the leaders of that attempt, as well as his known anti-Nazi sentiments, served as sufficient grounds for his arrest and execution. The letter that follows was written to his mother the night before he was executed.

Berlin, October 11, 1944. Evening

My own beloved Mama:

Today for a very special reason the notion came to me to write you once again, although a short letter to you is enclosed with my previous letters of farewell. I have no fear at all. Father used to tell me that our grandfather on his deathbed refused a soothing medicine with the words, "Everything must be endured." He stood sovereign over death—it was quite magnificent.

For a week now I have been awaiting death from day to day; right now, for example, I expect it tomorrow. I take pleasure in the sunshine and I have tried to free myself from the world only insofar as I have given up reading and, as much as possible, keep my thoughts away from all political and military matters. Aside from thoughts about my little brood [his wife and two small children], I am a completely happy man—a phenomenon that has often been found astonishing here. . . .

Death now means nothing to me; yet how gladly would I have gone home *with* my little brood, whom I can no longer care for and protect. But whenever such earthly thoughts come to me, the Lord reminds me that according to human probability I should in any case not have been beside them in time of stress, and that, above all, He is a far better protection. . . .

I know that you will never abandon my dearest one [his wife] and that you will keep in mind especially her infinitely tender heart, which has such need of love and likewise holds all of you so dear. For this, and for all the boundless love of nearly forty-two years, I thank all of you, and especially you, my indescribably beloved mother, from the depth of my heart.

No child has ever received a richer or deeper love from his mother than

Your Allechi

With infinite gratitude I thought today of the splendid childhood that your love above all else made for me in Mitau and Wilkajen. Everything is in a golden glory, with you at the center.[8]

When a person was a Nazi victim, it did not much matter whether he was Junker or Jew. After the war, a few individuals

—inspired by the discovery of the farewell letter of Baron von Roenne—decided to make a collection of farewell letters of the Nazi victims. In the foreword to that volume, called *Dying We Live,* Reinhold Niebuhr, the eminent theologian, wrote: "This collection of farewell letters proves what a refining fire the flames of martyrdom are. Non-German readers will learn from reading these letters that it is impossible to indict a whole nation and that in the same nation which generated and succumbed to Nazism there were the spiritual resources which made these heroic lives and deeds possible." In the great counterbalance of life, these fragile missives, containing ephemeral and lofty thoughts on thin and torn paper, have had to serve as the best available antidote for the unspeakable barbarities that prompted their writing.[9]

A collection of letters of a similar genre—written before execution—is *De Sidste Timer (The Last Hours).*[10] It is a book of letters written by Danish patriots—members of the Danish resistance movement—on the night before they were executed by the Nazis, who were then occupying their country.

Kim Malthe-Bruun, a young Danish seaman, was shot by a firing squad on Sunday, April 8, 1945. A few weeks after his arrest, in December 1944, he wrote the following letter, which was smuggled out of prison and delivered to his mother. He was twenty-one years old.[11]

> . . . The Gestapo is made up of very primitive men who have gained considerable skill in outwitting and intimidating feeble spirits. . . .
>
> Now listen, in case you should find yourself someday in the hands of traitors or of the Gestapo, look them—and yourself—straight in the eye. The only change that has actually taken place consists of the fact that they are now physically your masters. Otherwise they are still the same dregs of humanity they were before you were captured. Look at them, realize how far beneath you they are, and it will dawn upon you that the utmost that these creatures can achieve is to give you a few bruises and some aching muscles. . . .

Confront them calmly, showing neither hatred nor contempt, because both of these goad their overly sensitive vanity far too much. Regard them as human beings and use this vanity against them.

Your Kim

This same brave young seaman wrote a letter to his sweetheart that is practically a rutter for her survival, in which he uses rutter-like language: "But one day a storm tore us asunder; I struck a reef and went down, but you were washed up on another shore . . ." The young philosopher enjoins his beloved to read Plato so she might know of the love he feels for her. The letter is dated April 4, 1945.

My own little sweetheart: Today I was put on trial and condemned to death. What terrible news for a little girl only twenty years old! I obtained permission to write this farewell letter. And what words shall I write now? How shall they, my swan song, sound?

We sailed upon the wild sea, we met each other in the trustful way of playing children, and we loved each other. We still love each other and we shall continue to do so. But one day a storm tore us asunder; I struck a reef and went down, but you were washed up on another shore, and you will live on in a new world. You are not to forget me, I do not ask that: why should you forget something that is so beautiful? But you must not cling to it. You must live on as gay as ever and doubly happy, for life has given you on your path the most beautiful of all beautiful things. . . .

I think of Socrates. Read about him—you will find Plato telling about what I am now experiencing. I love you boundlessly, but not more now than I have always loved you. The stab I feel in my heart is nothing. That is simply the way things are, and you must understand this. Something lives and burns within me—love, inspiration, call it what you will, but it is something for which I have not yet found a name. Now I am to die, and I do not know whether I have kindled a little flame in another heart, a flame that will outlive me; nonetheless I am calm, for I have seen and I know that nature is so rich that no one takes note when a few isolated little sprouts are crushed underfoot and die. Why then should I despair, when I see all the wealth that lives on?

Lift up your head, you my heart's most precious core, lift up your head and look about you. The sea is still blue—the sea that I have loved so much, the sea that has enveloped both of us. Live on now for the two of us. . . . Remember, and I swear to you that it is true, that every sorrow turns into happiness—but very few people will in retrospect admit this to themselves. They wrap themselves in their sorrow, and habit leads them to believe that it continues to be sorrow, and they go on wrapping themselves in it. The truth is that after sorrow comes a maturation, and after maturation comes fruit. . . . I should like to breathe into you all the life that is in me, so that thereby it could perpetuate itself and as little as possible of it be lost. That is what my nature demands.

Yours, but not forever,

Kim

Oftentimes, last letters are concerned with creeds, moral crusades and political causes. The letter of John Brown is such an example. He was a condemned prisoner of war in a conflict which he had tried to start. He had put the torch to the enemy. The enemy was slavery. He was not a bandit in the ordinary sense; he was a single-minded and zealous crusader.

Brown was a fanatical and religious abolitionist. He appeared settled only in relation to his beliefs; much of the rest of his life was chaos. He moved from Ohio to Pennsylvania to Massachusetts to a Negro community in New York to Kansas to Virginia. He had twenty children (by two wives), and in effect, together with fewer than two dozen men (including some of his own children), formed a small army of his own. He believed that he had a sacred mission. In May 1856, he, four of his sons and three other men attacked a cabin of proslavery settlers on the Pottawatamie River in Kansas, and hacked five of them to death.

In the summer of 1859 he and twenty-one others moved to

a farmhouse near the federal armory at Harpers Ferry, Virginia. He attacked and captured the armory on October 16, but two days later a force of soldiers under Colonel Robert E. Lee overpowered his group, killing ten of his men, including two of his sons.

Brown was tried for murder, fomenting slave insurrection and treason. He refused to plead guilty; he also rejected an opportunity to plead insanity. At his trial he said: "I believe that to have interfered as I have done—as I have always freely admitted I have done—on behalf of His despised poor, was not wrong, but right." He was convicted, and was hanged on December 2, 1859. He wrote the following rutter-like letter on the eve of his execution.

Charlestown Prison, Jefferson Co., Va.
30th Nov 1859

My Dearly Beloved Wife, Sons; & Daughters, Everyone

As I now begin what is probably the last letter I shall ever write to any of you; I conclude to write you all at the same time. I am waiting the hour of my public *murder* with great composure of mind, & cheerfulness: feeling the strongest assurance that in no other possible way could I be used to so much advance the cause of God; & of humanity; & that nothing that either I or all my family have sacrificed or suffered: *will be lost*. . . .

Oh do not trust your eternal all upon the boisterous Ocean, without even a *Helm;* or *Compass* to aid you in steering. I do not ask any of you; to throw away your reason: I only ask you, to make candid & sober use of your reason: My dear children will you listen to the last admonition of one who can only love you? Oh be determined at once to give your whole hearts to God; & let nothing shake; or alter; that resolution. You need have no fear of *regretting* it. . . .

Be determined to know by experience as soon as may be: whether Bible instruction is of Divine origin or not; which says; "Owe no man anything but to love one another." John Brown writes to his children to abhor with undying hatred also: that "sum of all villainies;" Slavery.

Remember that "he that is slow to anger is better than the mighty: and he that ruleth his spirit; than he that taketh a city." Remember also: that "they that be wise shall shine; and they that turn many to righteousness: as the stars forever; & ever." And now dearly beloved Farewell. To God & the word of his grace I commend you.

Your Affectionate Husband & Father
John Brown[12]

There is a curious prophetic quality to John Brown's death. He welcomes it as a martyr, believing that it is only a single incident in his long crusade. At his trial he said: "I submit to arrest knowing full well that I shall be hanged for this attempt to end the evils of slavery. But after I am dead the evil will remain and you and all other patriots will come to learn that it can be purged from this guilty world only with blood." Prophecy, maybe; certainly not the language of flexibility and arbitration. The word "blood" is especially frightening. With a prescience of his own, he is warning us of the civil war to come.[13]

In 1977, exactly fifty years after the controversial execution of Nicola Sacco and Bartolomeo Vanzetti, the Lowell papers on that case were opened at the Harvard library. The letters revealed a number of interesting facts about the handling of their case. A. Lawrence Lowell—his name combines the names of two Massachusetts mill towns associated with his family—had been president of Harvard and, together with the president of the Massachusetts Institute of Technology and a former probate judge, had been appointed to an advisory committee to the governor of the commonwealth to advise him whether to grant clemency to Sacco and Vanzetti. In spite of evidence that both of the accused were not at the scene of the robbery-murder when the crime was committed and much other evidence that others were guilty, the governor refused to grant clemency and his advisory committee agreed that the trial had been fair. Public opinion was hostile to the defendants—there was a "Red scare" in the air and the two defendants were seen as aliens, agitators, anarchists and, worst of all, atheists. In the end, President Lowell voted his class ties and seemed indifferent to the shaky evidence and the unfair conduct of the trial.

Sacco had been working in a shoe factory; Vanzetti was a fish peddler. Both had come from Italy in 1908. The robbery and murder occurred in 1920. The trial and appeals dragged on for seven years, until both men were electrocuted just after midnight on August 21, 1927. The day before his death, Vanzetti, an unschooled immigrant, wrote this letter, which was published almost immediately and is now a part of our American legacy, to Sacco's son.

August 21, 1927. From the Death
House of Massachusetts State Prison

My Dear Dante:

I still hope, and we will fight until the last moment, to revindicate our right to live and to be free, but all the forces of the State and of the money and reaction are deadly against us because we are libertarians and anarchists.

I write little of this because you are now and yet too young to understand these things and other things of which I would like to reason with you. . . .

I tell you now that all that I know of your father, he is not a criminal, but one of the bravest men I ever knew. Some day you will understand what I am about to tell you. That your father has sacrificed everything dear and sacred to the human heart and soul or his fate in liberty and justice for all. That day you will be proud of your father, and if you come brave enough, you will take his place in the struggle between tyranny and liberty and you will vindicate his (our) names and our blood. . . .

I would like you to also remember me as a comrade and friend to your father, your mother and Ines, Susie and you, and I assure you that neither have I been a criminal, that I have committed no robbery and no murder, but only fought modestly to abolish crimes from among mankind and liberty for all.

Remember Dante, each one who will say otherwise of your father and I, is a liar, insulting innocent dead men who have been brave in their life. Remember and know also, Dante, that if your father and I would have been cowards and hypocrits and rinnegetors of our faith, we would not have been put to death. They would not have convicted a lebbrous dog; not even executed a deadly poisoned scorpion on such evidence as they framed against us. They would have given a new trial to a matricide and abitual felon on the evidence we presented for a new trial.

Remember, Dante, remember always these things: we are not criminals; they convicted us on a frame-up; they denied us a new trial; and if we will be executed after seven years, four months and seventeen days of unspeakable tortures and wrong, it is for what I have already told you; because we were for the poor and against the exploitation and oppression of the man by the man. . . .

The day will come when you will understand the atrocious cause of the above written words, in all its fullness. Then you will honor us.

Now Dante, be brave and good always. I embrace you. P.S. I left the copy of an American Bible to your mother now, for she would like to read it, and she will give it to you when you will be bigger and able to understand it. Keep it for remembrance. Good-bye Dante.

Bartolomeo[14]

What we particularly notice about many of the foregoing letters, especially when we contrast them with suicide notes, are the ties to loved ones. A Danish psychiatrist, Frederick Wagner, has also observed this striking difference between suicide notes and letters of farewell. He pointed out that in a farewell letter one finds a great love of relatives; that the writers, in their last written words, stick to life and "reveal a positive, dignified, often religious attitude toward life and a warm attachment to the family."[15]

Here is a more recent example, from another place. Vladimir

(Vlado) Clementis, who had been minister of foreign affairs for Czechoslovakia in 1948, joined the Czechoslovak Communist Party when he was a university student. He served as a Party representative in parliament in the 1930s. He was recognized as having a keen mind; he had studied law, philosophy and political science and was fluent in several languages. In 1945 he was appointed secretary of state; in 1948, after Jan Masaryk's mysterious death—he was apparently thrown out of the window of the Czech foreign office by the Russians—Clementis was appointed minister of foreign affairs for Czechoslovakia.

In the late 1940s and the early '50s, in the last years of Stalin's life (he died in 1953), a wave of anti-Semitism swept anew through the Soviet states. Because of the influence of Soviet policies, the Jews serving in the Czechoslovak Communist Party leadership posts lost their positions and were arrested. The low point of that era was the trial, in 1951 and 1952, of Rudolf Slansky, the former secretary general of the Party and vice premier of the country. He and ten of his Jewish associates were tried on political charges, were found guilty and were executed. Clementis, who was not Jewish, was included in this group, apparently to give the trial an other than blatantly anti-Semitic appearance. He was imprisoned in January 1951, found guilty of crimes against the state in what have come to be called the "Slansky trials" and was hanged on December 3, 1952. (His ashes were then strewn from a truck through the streets of Prague.)

Here, from Eugene Loebl*—who was imprisoned for several years as a result of a conflict with the Soviet minister of foreign trade—are some details of Clementis's arrest.

"In November 1949, I learned that Clementis [then serving as the United Nations delegate from Czechoslovakia] had un-

*This account and all the Clementis letters that follow were given to me personally by Eugene Loebl.[16] Clementis's letters were published in 1964 in Prague by the Publishing Company of Political Literature under the title *Listv z vazeny (Letters from Prison).*

dergone a series of confrontations with the Soviet representative to the U.N., Vishinsky. Soon after, news of his impending imprisonment was leaked to the Western press. Clementis contacted the Canadian minister of foreign affairs, Lester Pearson, requesting asylum from the Canadian government. A meeting was arranged by the Soviets with Clementis's wife, Lida, who was then in Prague. Lida was a beautiful and fragile woman who had had a brief career as an opera singer. She was asked to inform her husband that the rumors regarding his imprisonment were false, and thus deceived, she flew to New York to meet Clementis, who was reassured, and returned to Prague.

"Clementis was imprisoned in January 1951. Knowing how much Clementis cared for his wife, the interrogator threatened to imprison her should he not confess to the charges. Because they believed that Lida might commit suicide before Clementis capitulated, the interrogators imprisoned her anyway on the same day, without ever informing Clementis. Both Lida and Clementis were placed in solitary confinement, three cells apart from one another, on the same floor of the same prison. Lida was permitted to write to her husband only as long as she pretended that she was free and on the outside. He never learned of her plight, assuming during his entire imprisonment that she was living with her parents."

Here is a selection of Clementis's letters to his wife and one of hers to him—all written from prison cells, literally down the hall from each other, neither prisoner knowing where the other was. The letters glow with the fire of human courage under stress.

> To my dear Hadicka [Lida] and all my loved ones:
>
> I received permission to thank you for the thousand crowns that Father sent. I used the money to purchase some Pazyzans [cigarettes], pipe tobacco, and some other small items.
>
> I cannot tell you how much your message meant to me. It seemed as if it came from another distant world. Hopefully, I will

soon be allowed another letter from you. I yearn for it so much that I am afraid to hope.

Don't worry about my health. I am busy reading books from morning until darkness falls. Reading is "spiritual anesthesia" against what I have been experiencing here. It is amazing that in complete isolation from everyday life, one is sometimes able to sustain one's pervading interest.

I embrace you with love, my dear. Remember me to all.

Your
Vlado

In this next letter, Lida concocts news of the outside. She invents stories about Brocek, Vlado's favorite dog, who was also imprisoned by the authorities, in the same prison.

January 16, 1952

My dear beloved Vlado:

Thank you for your very dear letter—I longed tremendously for it, as I long for you. When I read your lines, your face appeared before me. I can imagine how you live and think from your words. I look forward to the time when you will write again, in a cheerful tone. . . .

All of us and those in Tisovec send their regards to you, and think of you often. We did not celebrate the holidays in your absence. Everyone is fine—Olga has had some trouble with her teeth, Mother with her legs, and various seasonal colds. Brocek is merry, lively, and very disciplined, though he runs without a leash. He has many lovers, and even a bride named "Rita." She resembles him, but is much younger. In the dining room, Brocek is allowed to sit on the table. This is his observation post: he waits to see if the "master is coming." Everyone is fond of him.

Jaraska Vasek's wife is nearly due to have her baby. Everyone is very curious, and awaits the event with great expectation. My parents are eager to meet their first grandchild. . . .

Please write soon. I am worried about your health, which you did not mention in your letter. To me, that is the most important thing. Write to me when you think most of me, and when you are melancholy. Our reliable telepathy will intervene, and offer you comfort. I think of you constantly—from the moment I rise, through the day, and late into the night. Can you see the sky? I will tie my messages to every cloud, the moon, and each star, so that they can carry my thoughts to you. I envy them.

I, too, would like to write love letters, after nineteen years of marriage. But I do not have the words to describe everything that I feel, of the depth of those feelings. When we are together again, we will make it up to each other. For now, we must try to learn from the "hard reality" of which you spoke. We must have faith that however difficult and bitter the present is, everything will again be well, everything will be put in order, and we will be happy once more. Despite all the pressures which I naturally feel, I am optimistic and have retained my faith. It is my intuition, my good premonitions, that give me faith.

Don't be unhappy, my dear. Be brave and write when you most think of me. Please tell me how you are feeling; if anything troubles you. Your dear ones send their warmest greetings. They all look forward to a happy reunion with you. You cannot know how we long for you.

With passion and love, I embrace and kiss you, my dear Vlado.

Your
Lida

June 27, 1952

My dear beloved Lida:

I would have to write in epic fashion to indicate how much your letters mean in this life of mine. This is particularly true of your last letter, in which I read and felt your very somber resolution to master the hardships we will have to face in the future. To think about the future—especially how it will affect you—is one of the most painful experiences I have known. It therefore means so much, so much to me that you have decided to endure the coming difficulties with new strength and new hope. Don't be concerned that you didn't answer my letter as well as you might have wished. I always find in your letters that which I am looking for, and that which I need, my dear Lida. . . .

Concerning my physical health—everything important is all right. I greet our dear ones heartily, and embrace and kiss you.

Your
Vlado

December 2, 1952

My dear and only Lida:

As I told you a few moments ago, I am at peace with myself. Yet until I saw you*—and I relived everything that has bound us to each other (and will bind us forever)—my peace of mind would have been achieved only by reason and will. My calm was full and pure, when you told me that you know and understand everything—I knew it couldn't be any different—I never doubted that you did. Nevertheless, your words were exactly what I most needed. Before seeing you, I wrote in a letter to Olga and Boza that the most difficult moment of my life would be to say farewell to my dear Lida. I won't rewrite that letter, though I expressed myself with hopeless inadequacy.

You know I have always been afraid of dramatic words. Yet what words could be dignified enough to express what your eyes told me? We were never so close as we were behind those bars of netted wire. How you must have suffered! You were so beautiful, and pure, and magnificent when you gave to me what I could not express, what I now feel.

I believe that you shall have the endurance you will need for the difficult life which awaits you; this is for me a great comfort and final consolation. I know that you will find the answer to the question you asked me and which I felt unanswered: "How to live." You can only live a life of dignity; the life of someone who was and remained till the very end in my thoughts, the goal and meaning of my life.

I believe that you will witness—in 10–15 years?—a Socialist Europe; that you will greet it for me. For this reason, too, you mustn't lose hope. You must cultivate a positive relationship with

*The Russian authorities permitted the two to see each other—with a screen between them—the day before Clementis's execution.

our times and with life itself. You know better than anyone else who and what I was; how I felt and thought; what was the nature of my shortcomings and mistakes, and as a result, my bad deeds and behavior. In a world free of tension, of danger, of unexpected change, and the sultry atmosphere of discord, I know that others, too, will see and comprehend. . . .

I smoke my last pipe. I listen and hear you sing the songs of Smetana and Dvořák. I am and shall always be with you.

Your
Vlado

In 1963, more than ten years after Clementis's execution, a transient groundswell of liberalism became apparent in Czechoslovakia. Due to this changing political climate, Clementis's case was reviewed and he was declared "rehabilitated."

The day after her husband's death, Lida was released from prison. She gave the letters, hers and her husband's, to Loebl, who brought them to the United States. He states that she was a broken woman; that she could not fully accept that her husband was dead. He reports her saying, "I cannot believe that the Party could have done this to Vlado, a man who dedicated his life to Communism." He learned later that she was being treated in a mental hospital. He says, "What happened subsequently [after 1968] I do not know."

Sometimes (but very infrequently) the person scheduled to be executed is, at the very last moment, reprieved. Here, below, is a most unusual after-reprieve letter, written in 1849, by one of the most profound creative artists of the nineteenth century. Fiodor Dostoevsky had been arrested and condemned for being part of a revolutionary political group. The letter was written to his brother the day after Dostoevsky's sentence of death was commuted by the czar—a decade before he was to write his world-famous books. But the very titles of some of those books—*The House of the Dead, Notes from the Underground, Crime and Punishment*—tell us that the memories of those terrible moments when he looked into the abyss were never far removed from the center of his creative consciousness. For a few seconds in his life, he had been suspended precariously between life and death. His American contemporary Melville wrote in one of his early novels, "Oh soul! thou then heardest life and death."

So must Dostoevsky have suffered as he was led out to be shot. To such a man, so cruelly treated and so capriciously reprieved, life is then a bonus, especially dear, almost unreal, a haunted and chance affair (like the throw of the dice), and forever after, both death and resurrection sit, like two perverse imps, one on each shoulder, and life is a gamble. (Dostoevsky became heavily addicted to gambling).

The Peter and Paul Fortress
December 22, 1849

Mihail Mihailovich Dostoevsky
Nevsky Prospect, opposite Gryazny Street
in the house of Neslind

Brother, my precious friend! All is settled! I am sentenced to four years' hard labor in the fortress (I believe, of Orenburg), and after that to serve as a private. Today, the 22nd of December, we were taken to the Semionov Drill Ground. There the sentence of death was read to all of us, we were told to kiss the Cross, our swords were broken over our heads, and our last toilet was made (white shirts). Then three were tied to the pillar for execution. I was the sixth. Three at a time were called out; consequently, I was in the second batch and no more than a minute was left me to live.

I remembered you, brother, and all yours; during the last minute you, you alone, were in my mind, only then I realized how I love you, dear brother mine! I also managed to embrace Plescheyev and Durov who stood close to me, and to say good-by to them. Finally the retreat was sounded, and those tied to the pillar were led back, and it was announced to us that His Majesty had granted us our lives. . . .

Yes, it's true! The head which was creating, living with the highest life of art, which had realized and grown used to the highest needs of the spirit, that head has already been cut off from my shoulders. There remain the memory and the images created but not yet incarnated by me. They will lacerate me, it is true! But there remains in me my heart and the same flesh and blood which can also love, and suffer, and desire, and remember, and this, after all, is life. . . .

Can it indeed be that I shall never take a pen into my hands? I think that after the four years there may be a possibility. I shall send you everything that I may write, if I write anything, by God! How many imaginations, lived through me, created by me anew, will perish, will be extinguished in my brain or will be split as poison in my blood. Yes, if I am not allowed to write, I shall perish. . . .

Well, good-by, good-by, brother! I embrace you closely. . . . do not change, love me, do not let your memory grow cold, and the thought of your love will be the best part of my life. Good-by, good-by, once more! Good-by to all!

Your
brother

What these letters, written under the direst threats of enforced death, show us is the nobility to which the human spirit is capable of rising. We see that people can stand—sometimes shaken, sometimes unshaken—above adversity under the conditions of severest stress. These precious rutters show us that, by and large, when put to the ultimate test of a direct threat of death, the human spirit, *as victim,* does not fail. It is only when we act as perpetrators and as villains that we need to feel an unforgivable shame.

5

Malignancy: Dialogues with Life-Threatening Illnesses

> All are born with halters round their necks; but it is only when caught in the swift, sudden turn of death, that mortals realize the silent, subtle, ever-present perils of life.
>
> Herman Melville, *Moby Dick* (Chapter 60)

It is from Hippocrates, the great physician of antiquity, that we get the term "carcinoma." It comes from the Greek word *karkinos,* meaning crab. It is so called because the large veins surrounding a tumor look like the extended claws of a crab spreading its multijointed appendages over the tumor like so many hostile tentacles. What Hippocrates did not know (except maybe by prescience) is that a metastasizing cancer can reach, crablike, throughout the body, touching, malignantly, several organs at once.

Just as the "voice of the turtle"—the cooing of the turtle*dove*—was heard throughout the land in biblical times, so today the "voice of the crab," when it is understood to mean the voices of victims of cancer, is heard throughout the land. That voice, sometimes weak but usually clear enough, is worth listening to. Here is the sound of one of those voices.

> I'm giving up. I want it to be over. I don't expect any miracles anymore. The sweating and the fevers just get me down. And yet I feel good. It's going to be a slow process. Maybe not so much a painful process, but a slow process. I'd like to get out. And then I'd also like to go to sleep and die. I mean, I don't know what to say. I'm just tired. I woke up this morning, I was really frightened. I was saying, dear God, dear God, what am I going to do? Dear God, dear God, doesn't answer.

The words are those of Marion, a twenty-two-year-old professional dancer and a hairdresser, a young man dying of acute myologenous leukemia. I am at his hospital bedside. These quotations are verbatim from a cassette tape. His voice is low; the words are spoken softly, interrupted by his occasional coughs and sighs.

Initially, when he came to the hospital, his behavior was hostile and irascible—"bitchy," as one doctor later said to me. He railed at the nurses in a vituperative way, calling them foul names. The last straw for them was his throwing a full urinal at a nurse. Then I was asked by his doctor to see him. The very beginning of the first session was somewhat unusual: I went into his hospital room, gently touched his hand, addressed him by his first name and said that I understood that he had been a bad boy. It was a big chance to take; he might have been totally alienated by such an abrupt approach. He began to sob; we immediately had a binding psychological relationship.

His behavior on the ward calmed down within hours; he seemed only to need someone to meet him "where he lived," with his terror and anguish and pain. The session reproduced on these pages took place several weeks after the first one—I saw him almost every day—and occurred about ten days before he died. The session continued as follows:

Shneidman. What was that fear of?

Patient. Oh, the unknown and another day, another day. Something else to keep me going. *(Coughing)* Dr. Shneidman, if there was a way I could end it now I would do that. It's taking so long. I don't have much patience, I guess.

S. That's true. This is a trial for you in many deep ways, including that one.

P. Including patience, you mean?

S. Yes. I don't think there has ever been a time in your life that you've had to be so patient.

P. How do you do it? I'm scared. You said you'd say what death was.

S. Pardon me!

P. You said you'd say what death was. You said it was something that I wouldn't know anything about.

S. Yes.

P. If I could only be sure that it would be peaceful. Will it be peaceful?

S. I can guarantee it.

P. Because that's so important. It's almost more important than anything else, that it be peaceful. My mother still wants to believe that maybe something will happen.

S. In what ways have your relationships with your mother changed in the last several days?

P. I've loved her. I let myself love her. *(Weeping)* Without any ties. I let myself love her without feeling that she was going to emasculate me. I've let her love me. I've let her be a mother. She's been so beautiful. I get more comfort from her than from anybody else.*

S. That's beautiful. Do you think it took this state for that to happen?

P. I don't know. I know for me it has, because now there's no reason to be wary of her castrating tendencies because she really means well for me. And she brings me such comfort, and she's so selfless. Crying's not supposed to help. It hurts when you get a fever and you sweat a lot, which is what I do. . . . And if there is a God, if there is somebody that I knew I could pray to that maybe

*Only a few weeks before, he had refused to talk to his mother or even to permit her to come into his hospital room.

could perform this miracle, I'd be most thankful and I'd show it in every way I could. *(Coughing)* It's so far-fetched, so unreal. I don't have a chance. I want to live so much. I don't want to die now. I'm half there and I'm half here, maybe more than half there. Because I don't get any encouragement anymore about living from the doctors. Right now, the big thing is just doing as good a job as possible to keep me alive for as long as possible, which is something I really don't want to do. Because if it's over, shouldn't it be over? Shouldn't I be out of the way? My mother keeps saying take each day as it comes. It's very difficult, extremely difficult. I had a lot of trouble doing that before. I'm having even more trouble doing it now. . . . So many people have said how much I touched their lives.

S. I'm sure that's true.

P. All kinds of people, young, old, my contemporaries. I never knew it.

S. How does all that make you feel?

P. I went to bed last night after listening to it, hearing it, and talking about it. I went to bed last night feeling good, and it was very comforting. But then I woke this morning and I was in this terror. It's like I need constant reassurance that I've been a good person and that there's someone there to love me. I guess I don't call that much of a success.

S. How do you mean?

P. I suppose if I'd been that way, I should be much more capable of taking this thing.

S. With more calmness?

P. Yeah. Maybe even fighting it better. I haven't fought it very well. It's almost as if I've wanted to die, from the time I got it. Not wanted to die, but knew I was going to die.

S. Sort of gave in to it?

P. Yeah. . . . I remember a few months ago they did a blood test and a bone marrow and then the doctor gave me a shot which turned out to be Valium and then he told me I had leukemia.

S. How did he tell you? Did he preface it in any way?

P. I think he told me, he told me in a way that was like we caught it at a good time, that we really have a good chance, that they wanted me to go to the hospital.

S. What were your reactions?

P. I called my mother right away.

S. What went through your head? Did you know what that diagnosis meant?

P. *(Coughing)* I recognized the seriousness, but I was in a state of shock.

S. What did you say to your mother?

P. I told her I had leukemia.

S. What was her reaction to that?

P. She cried. . . . But I really thought I was going to be cured. I mean, they told me I was. They told me I had a really good chance. And they've tried everything. Now a perfectly good person with an awful lot to give is going to die. A young person is going to die. The death is going to be absolutely senseless.

S. You say it in such an objective way about yourself.

P. It is a senseless death. I've asked the same question: why me? I don't get any answers. I suppose if somebody has to get it, it's just a disease and there's statistics and somebody has to get it, so maybe a friend of mine who's sailing along very nicely now thinking how sorry he is for me is going to get killed in an auto accident, because somebody has to get killed in an auto accident.

S. That's an interesting idea, like there's so much misery and so much death and it has to be distributed.

P. Yeah. I wish I could sleep, get some rest, but I dwell so much on it, on the dying. But if I get out I don't want to sleep. I want to get out. I want to do some things, just some things, maybe have a French meal, go to a movie, sleep with my lover again. In a way, though, it might make it more difficult. But why not? Why shouldn't I do it? Why shouldn't I walk outside again? I wonder how much I've missed. Now it's irretrievable. Do you think it's a good idea, even if I'm not a hundred percent right, if the doctors say it's O.K. for me to go out, do you think it's a good idea for me to go?

S. Naturally. Don't you?

P. You know, I'm still sweating. I think it's part of the leukemia, my throat still bothers me a bit, my stomach still bothers me a bit.

S. Well, I'll put the question to you: what do you think?

P. I almost think that almost anything is better than just lying here in this bed. I hate to be a burden to people on the outside but I'll never be completely well. I'm really at a low point.

S. I know, and a difficult one.

P. A really low point. . . . Do *you* fear death?

S. Yes, of course. Why do you ask?

P. I was just wondering about somebody who is more or less a specialist in the area of death, how he felt about it.

S. Well, I'm as mortal as anybody. I think I'm very close to you. I don't like illness and pain, incapacity, uncertainty, all those things that you don't like.

P. *(Sigh)* I feel peaceful now.

S. I'll come to see you on Monday, around eleven o'clock.

P. I hope I'll be here. I mean, I hope I'll still be here physically.

S. That's a necessary requirement. I'll see you then.

In this dying scene certain themes appear which will come up again and again. These include the terror ("I was really frightened"); the unnerving reaction to severe pain ("like to go to sleep and die"); the pervasive uncertainty ("if there is a God"); the fantasies of rescue ("somebody . . . that maybe could perform this miracle"); the resolute aspirations ("I would look upon myself as a better man"); the incredulity ("It's so far-fetched, so unreal. . . . It is a senseless death"); the dramatically changing interpersonal relationships ("I've let her love me"); the deep feelings of unfairness ("a perfectly good person . . . is going to die"); the concern with reputation after death ("I don't feel like I'm making much of a tape for you"); and the fight against pain ("I'm giving up. I want it to be over").

These are some of the themes that occur, and recur, when one is terminally ill and (barely) living with the growing threat of death. They are human fantasies, thoughts and emotions—that is to say, they are universal human experiences—that are in us from infancy, but are brought out (in different combinations) when we are severely threatened by the specter of the dreaded unknown.

Although the themes are often the same, there is not *one* way to die. Each person dies in a notably personal way.[1]

In current thanatology there are those—notably Elisabeth Kübler-Ross[2]—who write about a set of five "stages" of dying, experienced in a specified order. My own experiences have led me to radically different conclusions, so that I reject the notion that human beings, as they die, are somehow marched in lock step through a series of stages of the dying process. On the contrary, in working with dying persons, I see a wide panoply of human feelings and emotions, of various human needs, and a broad selection of psychological defenses and maneuvers—a few of these in some people, dozens in others—experienced in an impressive variety of ways.

Loma Feigenberg, an eminent Swedish thanatologist at the Karolinska Hospital, puts it this way:

> Kübler-Ross, whose work and widely read book have unquestionably been of far-reaching importance for the "new" thanatology, has divided dying into stages of its psychological aspects. . . . This system rests on her impressions and she has not presented a proper study in which they are verified. The eagerness and satisfaction with which this division into five stages has been adopted in many quarters are remarkable. It is as though this regular sequence in the confusing variety of dying has given

> many people a sense of security and confidence.
>
> Avery Weisman wrote recently: "Schematic stages—denial, anger, bargaining, depression, acceptance—are at best approximations, and at worst, obstacles for individualization."
>
> Nor is the question of stages in dying simply of theoretical thanatological interest—it also has a bearing on practical clinical work with the dying. Whatever her intentions may have been, the fact remains that the stages of Kübler-Ross have come to be regarded as a check-list for the process of dying. Each stage is expected to follow the one before it in the given sequence. And if a patient clearly deviates from this pattern, one is now liable to hear from the hospital staff that his dying is "wrong."[3]

The emotional states, the psychological mechanisms of defense, the needs and drives, are as variegated in the dying as they are in the nondying, although they focus—understandably, given the life-threatening situation—on some of the less euphoric aspects of life. They include such reactions as stoicism, rage, guilt, terror, cringing, fear, surrender, heroism, dependency, ennui, need for control, fight for autonomy and dignity, and denial.

It is important for a potential helper to avoid seeing a dichotomy between the "living" and the "dying." Most people who are seriously ill with a life-threatening disease—unless they are in extended coma—are very much alive, often exquisitely attuned to the symphony of emotions within themselves and the band of feelings of those about them. To tell a person that he or she has cancer may change that person's inner mental life irretrievably, but it does not lobotomize that person into a psychologically nonfunctioning human being; on the contrary, it may stimulate that person to consider a variety of concerns and reactions.

Nor is there any natural law—as those who talk about acceptance as the final stage of dying would seem to assert—that an individual has to achieve a state of psychoanalytic grace or any other kind of closure before death sets its seal. The cold fact is that most people die too soon or too late, with loose threads and fragments of life's agenda uncompleted.

My own notion of the psychology of dying—leaning heavily on general personality theory and the careful, detailed long-term approach to the study of human behavior by Dr. Henry A. Murray[4]—is that each individual tends to die as he or she has lived, especially as he or she has previously reacted in periods of threat, stress, failure, challenge, shock and loss. In this context I can paraphrase the nineteenth-century German biologist Haeckel's famous dictum and say that, in a sense, *oncology recapitulates ontogeny*—by which I mean that, roughly speaking, the course of an individual's life while he or she is dying over time, say of cancer, duplicates or mirrors or parallels the course of the life during its "dark periods"; that is, one dies as one has lived in the terrible moments of one's life.

To anticipate how a person will behave as he or she dies, we look at neither the plateaus nor the highlights of the life, but we search, as an eminent cancer doctor has recently put it, "in the hollow of the waves." Dying is stressful, thus it makes sense to look at previous episodes in one's life that would appear to be comparable or parallel or psychologically similar. There are certain deep consistencies in all human beings. An individual lives characteristically as he or she has lived in the past; and dying is living. There are no set phases. People live differently; people die differently—much as they have lived during previous episodes in their lives that were, to them, presages of their final dying period. My assertion is that the psychological history of the individual while he has cancer mirrors or reflects that same person's psychological history, in comparable periods, throughout his lifetime.

A recent article by Dr. John Hinton[5] reports a study of sixty terminally ill cancer patients. The study inquired into the relationship of each patient's personality and state of mind before and during the illness. The results indicated that we need to know the individual's previous patterns of handling life's demands *in detail*—the dozens of ways in which an individual has been strong, long-suffering, aggressive, weak, passive, fearful, and all the rest.

Hinton's findings (although tentative) are thought-provoking:

> Facing problems: This is the quality of previous character described by the husband or wife to indicate that the patient was one who coped effectively with life's demands rather than avoiding issues. It does appear to influence the most during the terminal illness. The uniform trend was for those who had previously coped well to be less depressed, anxious or irritable and to show less social withdrawal. This was one of the more consistent significant findings in the whole study. . . . Past difficulties in coping also increased the likelihood of current depression and anxiety. . . . there is support for the frequent impression that a patient's previous manner of living influences the way he dies.

All this suggests that if one could know a great deal about the other person (over the span of the entire life), then one could make accurate statements about future behavior that would not be simply prediction in the ordinary sense but would be more like reasoned extrapolations from the individual's past patterns of behavior.

The stressful periods in one's life do not always relate to illnesses. They might be tied to failures or threats in one's career or love life, the welfare or well-being of one's loved ones. Many a husband has had elevated blood pressure at the time of his wife's surgery, and vice versa. Among some groups whom anthropologists have studied, there is a condition called couvade, in which the husband takes to his bed and experiences labor pains during the time that his wife is giving birth to their child.

In her brilliant book *Illness as Metaphor,* Susan Sontag, who herself has had cancer, has written about two diseases: tuberculosis (and the curiously romanticized connotations that have been associated with that disease) and cancer (and the pejorative ideas that have accrued to it). She begins by invoking the image of two worlds—the world of the well and the world of the ill—in which illness is the night side of life, the more onerous citizenship. Sooner or later everyone is obliged, at least temporarily, to be identified as a citizen of the kingdom of the sick.[6]

To this compelling metaphor I would add yet a third kingdom: the world of the dying. There is a vast difference between being ill (feeling bad and having pain) and suffering from a life-threatening disease. There is an enormous psychological distance between being told one simply has an illness and being informed that one has a terminal inner enemy. "Being ill" and "dying" are quite different. When your life's passport has been stamped "Dying," it is like having it revoked—and it means that your capacity to travel, even back to the land of "just being sick," has been terminated.

In an intensive interpersonal exchange with a dying person, the focus is special. In this situation, the eye is on the calendar. The dying person usually introduces the topics of death and dying; the helper should not run from them. Conscious and unconscious meanings are sometimes blurred by the irrationality of death itself.

As I think of my own psychotherapeutic work with dying persons, it seems to me that I have been guided by the following principles, goals and beliefs:[7]

1. *The goal of increased psychological comfort.* The main goal of working with the dying person—in the visits, the give-and-take of talk, the advice, the interpretations, the listening—is to increase that individual's psychological *comfort.* One cannot realistically be Pollyannish or, sometimes, even optimistic; the helper begins in a grim situation which will probably become even grimmer.

2. *The autonomy of the individual.* This idea is based on respect for the individual. The opportunities to control one's own treatment, to maintain a sense of dignity and to be as free as possible of unnecessary pain[8] should not be snatched from a person simply because he or she is dying. People should not be

reduced to patients; their status as citizens and as human beings should be maintained.

The next document is by a university professor* with amyotrophic lateral sclerosis (ALS), a life-threatening neuromuscular disease. In "Notes of a Dying Professor" and "More Notes of a Dying Professor," he related some of his bitter experiences[9]—his shattering interactions with doctors and hospital personnel—and his reflections on (and implied criticisms of) the manner in which he was treated.

> After his cursory examination I began to realize that he was becoming increasingly non-communicative. And that alarmed me. What is he not telling me? And he became very grave and serious in his general demeanor. I asked him what he thought it was, but could get no reply. . . . He then let me know that I should see a neurologist immediately. . . . The neurologist was cold, aloof, highly efficient. . . . there began the growing sense from him that this was something serious. . . . I kept pressing him for a response but there was absolutely no response at all. And the non-verbal response, the avoidance itself generates considerable anxiety, fear and confusion on the part of any patient in that kind of situation.
>
> I felt treated as an object. Being a patient is one thing, but being an object is even less than being a patient. And I began to feel not only the fear of this unknown dread thing that I have, that nobody knows anything about—and if they know, they're not going to tell me—but an anger and resentment of "Goddamn it, I'm a human being and I want to be treated like one!"

Consider, in this case, what modern medicine has done. It lets us know almost as soon as possible (in ways ranging from the inadvertently cruel to the sympathetically "very regretfully") that we have a truncated period to live. It places over our heads a sword of Damocles with a time device that will cut the life

*The late Archie J. Hanlan, Associate Professor of Social Work, University of Pennsylvania.

string, and then it conscientiously devotes its considerable scientific energies to saving our somatic selves, while often, at the same time, but with no malice, either disregarding our deepest needs or otherwise unwittingly traumatizing our personalities and psyches.

The saddest part of this paradox is that it need not occur. Medicine could (and should) do both: it could treat the soma and at the same time unfailingly interact in a psychologically supporting way. In theory at least, except for the doctors' own possible neuroses, there are no persuasive reasons why doctors cannot recognize their patients' terrors and anxieties and insecurities in stressful situations, communicate so as best to allay those anxieties, and generally interact with their patients—putting aside the cloak of the mystique of the medicine man—exactly as they would want a colleague to interact with them if they themselves had a grave illness.

You don't have to be anybody to die, and you shouldn't have to be highly placed in society to die well. It is obvious that one is more likely to die well if one has ego strength at the beginning of the trial and if one is lucky and has a good support system of loving people in one's life, and lastly, if that system (including especially the way in which the art of medicine is practiced on you) will let you.

3. *The importance of transference.* In any list of Freud's core ideas, the concept of "transference" would have to be included. That notion holds that human beings tend to relate to certain other "figures" in their lives—doctors, teachers, policemen, servants, etc.—in ways that mirror their own deep need for love, or fear of authority, or disdain for weakness, etc. These feelings and needs stem from their early unconscious reactions toward their own parents and siblings; that is, they have a built-in proclivity for quickly transferring rather important feelings to another person. Transference can be both positive ("I like you") or its opposite ("I dislike you").

Here is an extraordinary excerpt from a therapy session illustrating the concept of transference. The patient is a lovely woman in her fifties, dying (now dead) of metastasized cancer of the breast. Her positive transference to me was an obviously comforting force in her dying days. This session occurred on a day when there had been a heavy rainstorm.

P. It's good to be indoors. I don't want to stop coming just because of the rain. I don't want to cancel unless I absolutely have to. Because I think once you start canceling, you think, Well, I just don't feel well or I'm just too tired or something like that and just cancel.

S. Your coming here in this heavy rainstorm raises an interesting question which is appropriate to ask in this setting. What do you get out of these sessions?

P. I don't know. I kind of enjoy them. Talking about things that I haven't thought of for ages and ages. I don't seem to be quite as nervous as I was. Of course, I'm taking some Valium. And I like to hear your thoughts. Oh, then you make me think of things that I haven't thought of before. I don't know what I'm supposed to get from these sessions. I've never been in therapy. Comfort, I suppose. I don't know whether it's a combination of the drugs and seeing you, but I am more comforted.

S. I'll now ask a question that only a psychotherapist would ask: What do you think of me?

P. I think you're very kind and you're very easy to talk to, and when there are gaps and I don't have much to say, why, you fill them in with interesting things, like when I'm floundering. You don't expect too much of me. And then, I think you understand the way I feel.

S. Do you like me? [Yes.] Why is that?

P. All those things, I guess.

S. Do I remind you of anyone? I don't mean in appearance or superficials or dress or status. [No.] Well, you've attributed to me some admirable human traits. Never mind whether those attributions are realistic. There have been other people in your life who have had those same traits. Who comes to mind when it's put in those terms?

P. Well, I guess probably you're the person I come to see because I'm troubled, so I guess it would be my mother, that I went to when I was in trouble. I didn't go to my father particularly. We loved each other dearly but we weren't able to communicate, but I could communicate very well with my mother, on anything. And we had a very close relationship, mother-daughter and just friends. But I can still talk more freely in front of you about things. There are some things I'd be ashamed to tell Mother. . . . Mother was like my nurse, my nanny, she was everything combined. I loved her very, very much. She was so gentle and so easy to talk to and so understanding. And she talked to me too, if she had any problems, so we talked to each other as if we were contemporaries. I really don't know why Dad and I could never let down the barriers, because we were terribly fond of each other.

S. You were terribly fond of your father; you deeply loved your mother.

P. I didn't see Dad that much. He was often away on business. But Mother was always around, always there when I came home from school, from the time I was very little. I can't ever remember an occasion when she wasn't there.

S. So you had a feeling of safety all through your life—at least until recently. [Yes.] You were blessed; you had relatively few psychological traumas in your childhood.

P. I had practically none. The only time I can remember being mad at Mother—and you'll understand it wasn't exactly Mother's fault—was when Charles [her husband] was ordered overseas for military duty, and I remember that first night when I went back home and Mother came into my room to kiss me good night and I told her that I wasn't ever going to let this happen to my little girl; I wasn't going to take my little girl's husband away like that. I was crying and sort of accusing Mother. And I remember that I apologized later, I went to her room, because I realized that what I had been saying was stupid, that I wasn't going to let the war take my little girl's husband away and blaming it on my mother.

S. It's understandable that you would have at that moment seemed to blame your mother for that loss.

P. Why? Why did I do that?

S. Oh, for a rather simple reason. You had looked to her to give you everything and to protect you from everything. She had done an almost one hundred percent job. In your head you had an absolutely magical feeling about her. She could do anything. You were as certain of your mother's being there as you were of the sun's coming up. And even though you were an adult and married, you were still a little girl, as in some ways you still are. That's in everybody. We never outgrow those feelings. And in that irrational moment, when you were crying, your major premise was, Mother, you can handle everything. It discounts the fact that there was a world war going on.

P. And you failed me.

S. And that makes psychological sense in the unconscious even if it doesn't make conscious sense.

P. No, it certainly doesn't.

S. But that's how the mind works. That's one of the most psychologically honest moments in your life. And then you say, I didn't mean it, but what you really mean is that you didn't mean it consciously, you meant it unconsciously, and it's really a message that contains a great compliment to your mother, because it implies that she's omnipotent. That's a beautiful moment really. It makes absolute sense in that way.

P. Yes, it does now. It didn't make any sense to me at all, all these years—after I said it or even since—until just now. Now I understand it.

S. And me? What omnipotent thing do you expect from me?

P. To cure my cancer, I suppose. . . .

Along these same lines, here, from Vilhelm Moberg's Swedish classic work of fiction, *The Emigrants,* are the words that Anna, Karl Oskar's eldest and favorite child, calls out to him as she is dying of a ruptured stomach:

> It hurts to die, Father. I don't want God to fetch me if it is so painful. I want to stay home. Couldn't I stay home—please let me stay home! You're so big and strong, Father, can't you protect me so God can't take me? . . . I am so little. Would you like to die, Father? Do you want God to come and get you?[10]

In this moving passage we see that subtle but vital difference between the omnipotence that the child projects on her parents (and the patient on her therapist) as surrogates of the Almighty, and the *real* or unescapable omnipotence of Nature Itself or God Himself. And we also see the implied threat of the victim to the heretofore supposed omnipotent father (or therapist) that if you will play God, then the real God will punish you: "Do you want God to come and get you [too]?"

4. *The goals are limited.* There is an understandable underlying concern with "success" in the motivational system of any effective therapist. With a dying patient, the therapist must realign his notions of what he can realistically do for that person. It is a process that no matter how auspiciously begun or effectively conducted, always ends in death. We need to appreciate that very few individuals die right on psychological target with all their complexes and neuroses beautifully worked through. The therapist or helper needs to be able to tolerate incompleteness and lack of closure. No one ever untangles all the varied skeins of one's intrapsychic and interpersonal life; to the last second there are psychical creations and re-creations

that require new resolutions. Total insight is an abstraction; there is no golden mental homeostasis.

The goal of completely resolving life's problems may be an unattainable one. As Avery Weisman says, "The best death is one that an individual would choose for himself if the choice were possible." The dying person can be helped to put affairs in order—although everyone dies more or less psychologically intestate.

Because there are no specific substantive psychological goals (for example, *this* insight or coming to *that* understanding), *the* emphasis is on the relationship and on the helper's continued presence. Nothing *has* to be accomplished. The patient sets the pace, determining even whether or not the topic of death is ever mentioned—although, if permitted, it usually will be. The "method of successive approximations" is useful, in which a dying person may be permitted to say, over the course of many days, I have a problem, an illness, a tumor, a malignancy, a cancer, a terminal metastasis. Different individuals get in touch with their illness at various points of candor. As helpers, all of us tend to evaluate our own performance in relation to how much we have given comfort in the death of another. In our own minds, we ruminate that the death of a grandparent, or a parent, or a sibling or a friend or a patient, has gone well or poorly, and we feel different amounts of pride, guilt or shame, depending on the role that we ourselves played in that death. It is clear to me, for example, how I feel about Marion, the young man who died of leukemia, described earlier in this chapter.

When I think of Marion, I mourn his death and I have relatively good feelings about having helped him resolve many conflicts within himself and, best of all, having helped to reunite him with his mother. It was a beautiful experience for him and for his mother. It was the most important single thing that could have happened within the awful context of his dying.

My memories of another case are not quite that triumphant.

In fact, I have a sense of rather abysmal failure in one vital aspect of my work with a fifty-year-old woman who died of lymphosarcoma. Our close psychological relationship served to help her. But in my interactions with her I lost sight of a rule which I constantly attempt to teach to others: To work from the beginning with the important survivors-to-be. She had been divorced for years and did not even know (or care) where her ex-husband was; but she had a grown son—and she zealously (or jealously) kept me from talking with him. I met him briefly only once in her hospital room and she was embarrassingly rude to him. It is clear to me now that in spite of her implicit wishes to the contrary, I should have telephoned him and talked with him early in my contacts with her. You will know how keenly I feel about this when you learn that he died the day after she did. The facts, as nearly as I can learn them, are that he burned to death in his apartment from a fire caused by a short-circuit in his radio. The coroner called it an accident. But the ghastly timing of his death left me with an overwhelmingly uneasy feeling. There is no question but that I should have been in close contact with her only son from the very beginning of my work with her.

Here is a tender, almost humorous rutter for dying (not of cancer, but of the simple wearing out of the human body). It was written by a learned physician, pensive in the twilight of his own life. It is by Hans Zinsser, from his autobiography, called *As I Remember Him.* In the unusual paragraphs below, Zinsser is gently berating the various organs of his own body for finally letting him down—but one senses that he also is somehow tolerant of his whole process of catabolism and disrepair, knowing that it is a part of nature's course that this decline inexorably occurs.

> Here I am, *me* as always. My mind more alive and vivid than ever before; my sensitiveness keener; my affections stronger. I

> seem for the first time to see the world in clear perspective; I love people more deeply and more comprehensively; I seem to be just beginning to learn my business and see my work in its proper relationship to science as a whole; I seem to myself to have entered into a period of stronger feelings and saner understanding. And yet here am I—essentially unchanged except for a sort of distillation into a more concentrated me—held in a damaged body which will extinguish me with it when it dies. If it were a horse I was riding that went lame or broke its neck, or a ship on which I was travelling that sprang a leak, I could transfer to another one and leave the old vehicle behind. As it is, my mind and my spirit, my thoughts and my love, all that I really am, is inseparably tied up with the failing capacities of these outworn organs.
>
> Yet, . . . [to] continue apostrophizing in a serio-comic mood, poor viscera, I can hardly blame you! You have done your best, and have served me better than could be expected of organs so abused. When I think of the things that have flowed over and through you! Innumerable varieties of fermented hops and malt and of the grapes of all countries and climates . . . to say nothing of the distillates—Scotch, Irish, Canadian, rye, bourbon, and the yellowish moonshine, colored with chicken droppings from the Blue Hills; and gin, genuine and synthetic; Schliyovitz from the Balkans, Starka from Poland, and the vodka of the Steppes; creme de menthe and cacao, Marie Brizard, Cointreau and Calvados.
>
> No, no, my organs! I cannot feel that you have let me down. It is quite the other way around. Only now it seems so silly that you must take me with you when I am just beginning to get dry behind the ears.[11]

Those failing, "outworn organs" are the paradigm of the dying process. Cancer is simply a dramatic and painful acceleration of this catabolic curve. And as Zinsser says and as everybody knows, when the hardware of the body goes, it takes with it the mind—the psyche, the person as he introspectively knows himself. That is what death is: it is the stopping of the working of someone's mind. You can die but you can never experience death itself. There is death only for the survivor. As the eminent American scientist-philosopher Percy Bridgman said: "*I* am always alive."

What is striking about these relatively rare memoirs of terminal illness is how their writers wish to communicate not only love and concern, but also—in an almost obsessed way—to share thoughts about the disease and about the dying process itself. These thoughts include the effects of the disease, the ways in which they were told of it, the impact of the diagnosis, concern over the prognosis, and reflections on the dramatic changes in self-image created by the very label of the disease.

The following is from the preface of a book—*Stay of Execution*—that has had wide circulation. It was written by the well-known author and journalist Stewart Alsop:

> This is a peculiar book. I have two reasons, or excuses, for writing it. First I have myself quite often wondered what it would be like to be told that I had an inoperable and lethal cancer, and I suspect a lot of other people have wondered the same thing. If a writer has had an unusual experience likely to interest a good many people, he has an instinct, and perhaps even a duty, to write about it. Second, after I had been told my remaining span of life would be short, I began to think back quite often about the life behind me. . . . In a way, no experience has been more interesting than living in intermittent intimacy with the gentleman W. C. Fields used to call "the man in the white nightgown" and whom I have come to think of as Uncle Thanatos, and sometimes, when I had been feeling very sick, as dear old Uncle Thanatos. Death is, after all, the only universal experience except birth, and although a sensible person hopes to put it off as long as possible, it is, even in anticipation, an interesting experience.

By the very title of Alsop's book he reminds us of the trauma of others for whom a fatal sentence of death has been ordered, seemingly mercifully lifted and then inexorably enforced. What seemed like a reprieve was only a postponement. Further, in that title Alsop implies a basic question, and in his text he explicitly raises it: Are the postponement and the temporary stay worth it? His veiled answer is partially contained in these paragraphs:

> What were the chances of successful remission?
>
> Better than 50 percent, he said. . . .
>
> How long would a remission last?
>
> "We have an AML [Acute Myelocytic Leukemia—the most common type of leukemia in adults] patient here in the hospital tonight," he said cheerfully. "He's been in remission for seven years. . . ."
>
> But what was the average?
>
> "About fifty percent of our patients with AML who go into remission last a year or more. . . ."
>
> How many died before two years?
>
> Dr. Glick hesitated a moment. "About ninety-five percent," he said, and briskly changed the subject . . .
>
> The night was a bad night. . . . I thought about what Dr. Glick had told me. . . .
>
> Would it really be worthwhile to spend a month or more cooped up all alone in a laminar flow room, losing my hair and my flesh, either to die in the room or emerge a bald skeleton and wait for death? Would it not be more sensible to reach for Hamlet's "bare bodkin," in the shape of a bottle of sleeping pills? And then a sense of the reality of death crowded in on me—the end of a pleasant life, never to see Tish or Andrew or Nicky or the four older children again, never to go to Needwood again, or laugh with friends, or see the spring come. There came upon me a terrible sense of aloneness, of vulnerability, of nakedness, of helplessness. I got up, and fumbled in my shaving kit, and found another sleeping pill, and at last dozed off.
>
> I never again had a night as bad as that night, nor, I think, shall I ever again. For a kind of protective mechanism took over, after the first shock of being told of the imminence of death, and I suspect that this is true of most people. Partly, this is a perfectly

> conscious act of will—a decision to allot to the grim future only its share of your thoughts and no more.
>
> The conscious effort to close off one's mind, or part of it, to the inevitability of death plays a part, I suspect, in the oddly cheerful tone of much of what I've written in this book. I instinctively preferred, for example, to recall episodes that had amused me during the war, like my first meeting with Tish, rather than the times when I was unhappy or afraid. In the same way, I remember from my career as a journalist those episodes that amused me, rather than those to which some profound meaning might be attached.
>
> The protective mechanism is also an unconscious reaction, I think. I remember seeing much the same process at work in combat. There is the first sudden shock of realizing that the people on the other side are really trying to kill you. . . . But, the incredulity soon wears off and a kind of unhappy inner stolidity takes over, coupled with a strong protective instinct that the shell or the bullet or the mine will kill somebody else—not me.
>
> In this way, the unbearable becomes bearable, and one learns to live with death by not thinking about it too much.[12]

In those paragraphs, Alsop, all by himself, seems to have rediscovered Freud's concepts of suppression, repression and denial. In his tender and insightful psychological writing, we see the appearance of the gyroscopic protector, the greatest of all of nature's anesthetics: denial—to push down in consciousness (into the unconscious of the mind) those thoughts and fears that might threaten to overwhelm us.

Let us now turn to another genuine death rutter—one written with the precise intention of being a guide for those who come after. It is by a young psychiatrist, dying of leukemia. (The document was given to me by his former mentor, Dr. Eugene Pumpian-Mindlin.) Here, with only a few emendations, is the young doctor's essay on his own dying.

> The idea of this essay was conceived in November but lay fallow until May of the following year [he died two months later]

because of my inability to delineate clearly both the objective and the content of this paper. The passage of time has, of itself, provided some jelling of the ideas and content which, for a time, were so amorphous and jumbled in my mind. My reasons for writing this paper are to objectify and clarify my own feelings regarding my illness, to help crystallize my perspective on matters of living and dying, and to inform others in a subjective way about the psychological processes that take place in a person who has a life-threatening disease.

A narration of the chronological events pertaining to my predicament is in order to keep the reader properly oriented. In November I discovered that I had acute myelogenous leukemia. This discovery was quite by accident and did not occur because of any perception of anything seriously amiss. I had noticed one evening that I had a number of petechiae [tiny blood splotches on the skin]. The following day I saw a physician who was a friend, and he recommended, after examining me and finding nothing unusual, that some blood tests be performed. This led to the ultimate diagnosis by bone marrow examination of the true picture. The next day the hematologist who had subsequently examined me and examined the slides of blood and bone marrow very reluctantly told me that I had this disease.

My initial reactions are difficult to describe and still more difficult to recall accurately. However, I do remember feeling that somehow the doctor's remarks could not be directed to me but must be about some other person. Of course, I shook off that feeling very soon during this conversation and as the full realization of the import of this diagnosis struck me, I was steeped in a pervasive sense of deep and bitter disappointment. I thought that I had been maliciously cheated out of the realization of all the hopes and aims that I had accrued during my professional career. I was in the third year of my psychiatric residency and on the brink of fully developing a professional identity. Further, and more important, I was also on the threshold of developing a true sense of personal maturity and personal identity. I felt now this would all be denied me and I would never live to realize the fruit of the struggles in which I had been engaged for so long a time.

I immediately went to see my department chief and discovered that he had already been informed. He was most kind and gracious and extremely helpful in setting my skewed perspective back on the right track. For that matter, from that moment onward I never wanted for good counsel and enormous equanimity and maturity from my supervisors and teachers, without whom I doubt I could have rallied as well as I did.

The next subjective feeling I can clearly identify is that I was increasingly apprehensive following the diagnosis about my inevitable decreasing body efficiency and thus very likely my decreasing efficiency and interest in my work. This engendered some little guilt over my anticipating not being able to do the job I had been doing. Indeed, because of the drugs it was necessary to take for the illness and not really because of the illness itself, the capability of my usual performance was sharply curtailed. Luckily when I expressed such feelings of guilt over not pulling my weight in the organization, this was immediately squelched by my teachers, who were able to assuage my unnecessarily hypertrophied super-ego, which has since become of a much more manageable size. Nonetheless, I did have pangs of remorse when I finally had to stop seeing long-term patients because my physical symptoms interfered too much with appointments. Surprisingly, I did not feel consciously angry or frightened by the knowledge that I had a life-threatening illness.

I was gravely disappointed and terribly annoyed that this thing inside my body would interfere with my life. But at no time did I really feel, as one might put it, "angered at the gods" for having such sport with me. Nor did I find that I used denial as a defense to any extent early in the course of the illness, as I did later on when it appeared that some of the chemotherapeutic measures were having considerably good effect and I began to feel that I could go on interminably from drug to drug and not die of my disease. Instead my attention was directed away from my illness in its early phases by some very practical matters which might be called "Setting My Affairs in Order." I was so busy with this that it served quite well to focus on an aspect of dying which is not connected with the disease process itself and thus considerably decreased my own anxiety. There was an enormous mobilization of energy to get things accomplished in this regard by both me and my wife.

There was a number of changes we needed to make in our lives in order to fulfill sooner than we had anticipated some of the expectations we had about how we would live. Although a great many things actually transpired, I shall mention only two or three here as examples. We first moved from a small rented apartment which was adequate for our needs at the time to a larger house and we purchased additional furniture. Because I was deeply interested in music and particularly in composing, we borrowed a grand piano from friends who were extremely gracious in allowing us to use it while they were living in the area and did not find as much use for it as they had in the past.

My wife undertook practically all of the details of this move herself and also redecorated one of the three bedrooms we had in the home so that I might have a private study and library. When we got all these things accomplished, we took stock of the situation and came to the realization that it had not really required a serious illness to do these things because we had not overextended ourselves in any financial sense and we could have done all this before I got sick if we had really set our minds on it. . . . We had, in effect, denied ourselves some of the comfort of a real home and space in which to work for no valid practical reason.

My parents expressed shock, grief and disbelief over the situation. They worried about such things as how does one get such an illness or, perhaps more cogently, why *should* one get such an illness, reflecting, I suppose, a very common fantasy that such a thing must be some kind of a punishment—just or unjust —visited upon the victim. When it came to the question of informing my three young children about my illness, I was met with the question based on the precept "How could you do this to them just before Christmas?" I explained that it was far better for the children to understand precisely what it was that was going on, rather than permit them to develop their own fantasies about it which could very easily be far worse than the truth. The fact that it was close to Christmas was quite beside the point.

As a matter of fact, it gave me an opportunity to clarify personally some of the confusion I was sure existed about the nature of this disease. Indeed, there were a number of fantasies, doubts and fears which very much needed to be dispelled. They were prepared to some extent for a not-very-well father who had an illness that might easily take his life in a short period of time. One common fantasy of all of the children (unexpressed except through probing) was, "Is this thing contagious? Will I get it if I am close to you?" As soon as this was corrected, the children found themselves able to be much closer to me. As it turned out later, nearly all of the children with whom I had therapeutic contact had this same fantasy.

Some of my colleagues may very well have had similar fantasies. If they did, I have not discovered it but can only surmise it because there have been practically no contacts at all with some of the people with whom I worked since the inception of my illness. There has been some speculation on my part (reinforced to some extent by conversations with supervisors) that some of the people with whom I have had fairly close contact in the past found it almost impossible to deal with me and my illness because of their own fears and fantasies concerning death.

One almost amusing idea came to light through one of my supervisors, namely that some of my colleagues might very well be wishing that I would drop dead and get it over with rather than continue to torment them as I was. For others there was a heightened awareness of a close relationship that had never been verbalized in the past. This occurred with two or three of my fellow residents and certainly we were all the better for it. Not only was there some clarification of feelings and a chance openly to discuss them between us, but also this produced a closer relationship.

At all times I tried to make it clear that I in no way wanted to avoid open discussion of my illness. I did not want to play any games of pretending that I was better than I was (although I am prone to do so), nor did I want to avoid responding to questions about how I was from day to day under the assumption that to be reminded of my illness might hurt me. On the contrary, I felt somehow annoyed if I was not asked how things were going with me because I wanted to share with others feelings about my illness. One of my friends and teachers commented that one of the things that bothered him most was the destruction of his fantasies of omnipotence by the knowledge of my illness. In other words, there was nothing he could do to change the situation, although he wanted to very much. I imagine that many of my fellow residents felt the same way and they responded to this in a very constructive manner. They were discussing this one day among themselves and one of them suggested they donate blood, which most certainly I would eventually need, as a means of doing something positive and relieving the terrible feeling that there was nothing that could be done. This was, I think, of enormous help to them and, of course, to me too.

I was also repeatedly assured by my division chief that I should assume only the work that I felt really capable of doing efficiently. He would rather, he said, that I did less than I had been doing and do a good job of that, than try to put in a full day and have to drag around looking rather dreary, reminding other people that I was sick. This made good sense to me, so I was able to stay home part of the time after I started to feel less well without feeling guilty about it. I have been enormously buoyed up by the generous support of the staff and I hope they know how deeply grateful I am to them. At this point I was feeling very dismal about my prospects for any longevity and I was very glad to get all the support that I did. I did not enter the hospital but continued working and began a program of medication as an outpatient. This was a very important step because otherwise I might have been compelled to concentrate almost exclusively on the internal workings of my disabled body and not been able to continue working. As it turned out, this was one of the most important features of the total adaptation to this disease, because everybody made me feel that I was not giving up, despite the reduction in the time I actually spent at work.

The relationship between me and my wife was also exceedingly important at this time. At first, of course, she responded with remorse, sympathy and total understanding. As time progressed and it appeared that I was evincing some durability and I was pretty much my old self despite the shadow I lived under, she was able to express some of the deeper feelings concerning me and my illness which were not really seen by her as separate entities. Since then we have been able to share feelings, more openly than ever before, never to the detriment of either of us. People wrongly assume that a sick person should be "protected" from strong, and particularly negative, feelings. The truth is that there is probably no more crucial time in a person's life when he needs to know what's going on with those who are important to him.

In the several months since the inception of my illness I became increasingly aware of a new sensitivity that had gradually but progressively developed in my interpersonal relationships, both with patients and with all my acquaintances. The sensitivity of which I speak is rather elusive insofar as a clear definition is concerned, but perhaps I can resort to describing it in terms of its effect. One thing I noticed most pointedly was that I was very much more tolerant of the vagaries and inconsistencies of other people's attitudes and behavior than I had ever been before. Perhaps "tolerant" is not a very good word. It might be better to use the word "understanding," because many times I have found myself perceiving very quickly what lay beneath a particular person's attitude or affect which did not seem altogether appropriate to the situation. Thus I found myself much more at ease with people whom I had found difficult to tolerate in the past. Some people commented they found it easy to be with me because I openly invited questions about my illness.

This heightened awareness of affect in others also extended to myself and I found that my own feelings were much more accessible to my conscious recognition than they had been in the past. I also found that all of my senses seemed more acute, though I believe that really I simply paid more attention to what was going on around me and, in a way, I found myself hungering for every sensory experience that I could absorb. In many ways the world seemed to offer more beauty and there was a heightened awareness of sounds and sights, which in the past I may have only casually observed or simply not have paid much attention to at all. Aside from the sensory and affective sensitivity which I had seemed to acquire, there appeared to me to be a culmination of all the learning experience that I had in my professional career, which, in a compressed space of time, became the foundation for practically a new way of life. Another way to put this is that there was quite suddenly an integration of all the values and understanding I had of human experience into some kind of cohesive whole which, although difficult to describe, made extremely good sense to me.

This brings me to a question which I had earlier put aside: What happened to all the anger and depression which should have occurred after the news of my illness? I think I know. It would seem that the struggles I had with myself had not been in vain and it was fortunate that I was where I was at the time all this happened, since I had a great deal of psychological help available to me. At any rate, it would appear that the peace I made with myself during my illness and the maturing ability that I was developing to cope with life crises like this one arose from several dynamic factors. One was the increasing capacity to sublimate the rage and aggression engendered by the impotency I felt regarding this invasion from within. Instead of striking blindly outwardly or, probably more likely, addressing the anger inward and thus becoming depressed, I became intensely involved in musical composition and composed practically like a madman for the first several weeks of my illness, completing one larger work and two smaller ones, which represented in that space of time more output in this field of art than I had ever been able to accomplish in the past.

This outlet proved so effective that it was very seldom that I was conscious of any feelings of despair or depression. Indeed, I suspect that when they began to reach consciousness I would begin furiously (and I use the word quite deliberately)

> to become creatively involved, and thus dispel the unpleasant affect. Certain instruments lend themselves to this kind of alteration in the discharge of affect better than others. For example, the percussion instruments, which in a sense include the piano, are really excellent ways to deal with the aggressive energy present in everyone. But it is revealing to cite the ways I thought of working with music in these past few months. I would attack the piano, I would literally hammer out a new piece.
>
> Certainly there are rewarding aspects of facing life-threatening illness. I have learned much about the alterations in my own internal psychological processes, and the subtle metamorphosis in interpersonal relationships which have occurred and are still occurring.
>
> By way of completing this little essay I might comment that in a way I have, at least intellectually, accepted and I hope that I can wholeheartedly embrace the idea that the death of an individual is really no more nor less than a punctuation mark in the endlessly fascinating conversation amongst all living things.[13]

Such a document is an unusual rutter because it describes the tone of a relatively calm voyage through admittedly stormy seas. It is a case where the enormously bad luck of leukemia falls on a relatively—up until then—lucky person: a physician, with a loving wife, an outlet in his music, and actively supporting supervisors and colleagues (and even patients)—in short, a person who has what is necessary for a good passage through the dying period: a strong support system. Consider even such details as the way in which he is treated by his physician and his department chief: "the hematologist . . . very reluctantly told me"; "my department chief . . . was most kind and gracious and extremely helpful." Those are tiny rays of the sun peeking through extremely dark clouds, which are sometimes just enough to make an absolutely gloomy time a little less intolerable.

The extraordinary public death from cancer of Hubert Humphrey can be a guiding example to some of one kind of "appropriate death." His published utterances about his cancer, his state of health and his death probably can stimulate many of us to think about our own way of dying.

Humphrey was an open man. (His autobiography is called *The Education of a Public Man.*)[14] Not only a gregarious man—"It was hard to tell where he left off and the people began," as Carl Sandburg had said of Lincoln—but also, in a pleasant sense, a man owned by the people. His dying was, in a remarkable way, a community experience. Toward the end, around Christmas time of 1977, he did not hide from the press or from his fellow citizens, but considering his state of health, gave rather freely and answered some pointed personal questions. It is the manner of his responding to these questions, the quality of his banter, his candor and his unique use of humor over the course of his illness that were special.

The insidious growth of Humphrey's cancer is now a matter of record.

> 1966–1968: First appearance of blood in urine (hematuria). Nonmalignant papillomas (small tumors) found in his bladder. Several removed over the next few years. No press announcements; no public utterances about his medical condition.
> 1973: A cancer-like tumor—a borderline or possible cancer found in his bladder. No press announcement.
> Late 1973: Radiation (x-ray) treatments, almost daily for six weeks. Not even his colleagues were aware of this.
> January 1974: First public disclosure of his serious bladder difficulties.
> September 1976: Another tumor found in bladder. First mention of cancer.
> Early October 1976: Surgical removal of his bladder (at the Memorial Sloan-Kettering Cancer Center in New York City).

Subsequent chemotherapy. Detailed newspaper coverage. Mid August 1977: Intestinal blockage. Colostomy performed at the University of Minnesota Hospital. Subsequent public announcement by his physicians of an inoperable pelvic tumor. His situation was then described as terminal.

January 12, 1978: A bulletin from his home in which he is described as noticeably weakened, but resting comfortably. His situation is listed as critical. The bulletin also stated that it was not planned that he would return to the hospital.

January 13, 1978: Hubert Humphrey died in Waverly, Minnesota.

Among Humphrey's public utterances about his own cancer, here is a typical remark which shows him not succumbing either to self-pity or to deep pessimism: "Deep down, I believe in miracles. They have happened to a lot of people who have been given up to die and then restored to health. If you don't overcome self-pity, the game is all over."

This is not to say that there were not moments of despair, but when Humphrey touched on those moments he separated them from everything else he said by using the word "honestly," by which he must have meant personally, candidly. In August of 1977, reflecting on his x-ray treatments in 1973, which had caused spasms in his bladder, he confessed: "I was in so much agony that I honestly wanted to give it up."[15] During that time he was secretly receiving treatments in the morning and going to his tasks in the Senate. Not even his Senate colleagues knew of his excruciating pains.

His public image was that of a fighter. On September 19, 1977, interviewed in Minnesota, he said, "I'm not ready to have somebody cover me up." But by then everybody knew that he was ailing and on a downhill course. On October 25, 1977, he returned to the Senate after an eleven-week absence during which he was hospitalized and operated upon and had permitted an announcement that he had an inoperable malignant pelvic tumor. On the Senate floor he responded to the affection of his colleagues. His remarks were emotional, sentimental, yet optimistic. The key words are "friendship" and "self-reliance": love of others flowing from inner strength.

> The greatest healing therapy is friendship and love, and over this land I have sensed it. Doctors, chemicals, radiation, pills, nurses, therapists are all very, very helpful. But without faith in yourself and your own ability to overcome your own difficulties, faith in divine Providence and without the friendship and kindness and generosity of friends, there is no healing.[16]

There was yet another characteristic nuance to Humphrey's public statements, especially those unprepared remarks in response to questions from reporters: it was the quality of humor; wry statements with double entendre. Here are two examples:

Late in 1977, after meeting privately with President Carter, Humphrey was asked what the two of them had talked about. His response included the remark that he had assured the President that he would not run against him in 1980. When one thinks about it, one immediately sees that it is a touching statement, said in a light-hearted but profound way.

The second example of this kind of buoyancy covering deeper and more lugubrious meanings occurred when he went home to Minnesota for the last time. This exchange took place, on December 23, 1977, at the Minneapolis airport:

Aide. Excuse me, we have time for one last question.

Reporter. Senator, do you want to scotch all those rumors about resignation?

Humphrey. Oh, I'm not resigning from anything. I may even join something. The [Senate] pay is good, the working conditions are good, and I like my associates. No, no, I have no intention of resigning. The only way that could happen is if I were totally incapacitated and I'm a long way from that, fellows. Have fun. Merry Christmas.

Photographer. Same to you, Senator, same to you. Hey, Senator, God bless you.[17]

Five months before Hubert Humphrey died, his doctors announced to the press—we must assume with his approval—that they had found a metastasized tumor that had spread to his pelvic bone; further, that the condition was medically inoperable, and that his situation was terminal. That announcement came from the University of Minnesota Hospital on August 18, 1977. Thereafter, the world either had to shun Humphrey as a leper and pariah (because of the social stigma of terminal cancer) or, because of who he was and the way in which he conducted himself, accept him as he was. The fact is, he was accepted and *pre*mourned—by President Carter at Camp David, by the entire Senate and by large segments of the populace—as perhaps no one else in American history has been. If, as Vice President Mondale said after Humphrey's death, he was an A-OK guy, Humphrey made it also A-OK to come out of the closet with cancer.

As important as Humphrey's providing a role model on how to die was the impact of his behavior on our ideas of the loathsomeness of cancer. In his dying months, he helped decontaminate cancer.

In his political and personal losses, Humphrey displayed both a certain realism and a touch of incredulity that never quite crossed over into incapacitating bitterness, and, withal, a certain buoyant optimism. In the end Humphrey was an undiluted winner.

The historic photograph (of January 15, 1978) of the assemblage behind Humphrey's catafalque in the rotunda of the Capitol—including Mrs. Humphrey, Carter, Ford, Nixon, Kissinger—shows many interesting facets. Among them is the deep contrast between the man who wanted to be President and the man who had beaten him for the presidency. It is a contrast that has only sharpened with time. There is Nixon, looking funereal and defeated, and the unseen Humphrey, nobly canonized within his coffin.

Humphrey salvaged some redeeming elements from his defeats by using his own special approach to the hollows in the waves of life. He saved for himself (and bequeathed to the rest of us) some worthwhile elements in his dying. There was a consistency in his living while he was well and his living when he was ill. But in Humphrey it is not so much the consistency we admire, as it is the style of it.

Humphrey did not lie to us about his cancer. He did not conceal from us its ravaging effects. We all knew that he wore a colostomy bag. But he did all this with a dignity and a good humor that absolutely undercut the baleful metaphors associated with that disease. In his openness and sharing, he helped change our notions of cancer itself. He is an important figure in the history of medicine.

Part Three

Mourning

6

Self-Mourning and Premourning: Preparations Before the Act

> I survived myself; my death and burial were locked up in my chest.
>
> Herman Melville, *Moby Dick* (Chapter 49)

Mourning is not a disease, but its deleterious effects are sometimes so crippling that it might as well be. The recently bereaved person is distressed and disorganized. Long-standing habit patterns of intimate responses with loved ones are irreparably broken. There is a gale of strong feelings, usually including those of abandonment and despair, sometimes touching on guilt and anger, and almost always involving a sense of crushing emptiness and loss.

Grief and mourning are such ordinary words that we each feel that we know almost instinctively what they mean, yet some further reflection will show that, even at the outset, one can distinguish at least three different kinds of mourning conditions. These are self-mourning (mourning for oneself as one is dying); premourning (mourning the loss of a loved one before that person has died, but after it is evident that the death is imminent); and mourning itself (the grief over the death of someone dear in one's life).

Much of human behavior anticipates some future event. When we cannot prepare ourselves, when we are taken unaware, then we are surprised and unnerved; that is, in part, what shock is. Thus it is not surprising that when we are faced by an inevitable loss (such as the death of a spouse who is dying of cancer), we would both consciously and unconsciously begin gradually to disengage, to deinvest, to inure ourselves to the hammer blows of the real loss before it occurs. That is what premourning is intended to do: to lessen the effects of the actual loss when it finally happens.

In self-mourning (or auto-mourning), the dying individual not only bewails the "naughtment" of the self after death, but, more usually, bemoans the partial losses that are being experienced in the present: inabilities to do things—to run, to walk, even to get out of bed—one could do before the life-threatening illness ravaged the strength and energies. These losses are incapacities: to perform, to cope, to enjoy, to experience in the world. One is gradually reduced to a living brain jailed in a failing body, locked within a bed, usually a hospital bed in a sterile and strange environment, and (whether at home or in hospital) often a bed of pain.

It is perfectly natural, then, to grieve at the losses that make one less than one used to be. And one is sometimes reduced to poignant wishes like: If only my stomach didn't hurt . . . If only I could get up and walk across the room . . . If only I could swallow . . . If only . . .

But mostly one grieves about one's memory bank. It is a shame for a mature and learned adult to take the mind's storehouse of memories and wisdom forever from the world, and it is not an act of untoward narcissism for a sensitive individual to grieve over this baleful certainty. Freud said that we cannot truly imagine our own death because, even in the imagining, we always remain as spectators. But that is not the whole story. As we imagine our own death—the world without us—we can be spectral spectators (like unseen ghosts), legitimately mourning because the world will be somehow less by virtue of our death.

An elegant, well-educated and thoughtful woman in her

fifties, under threat of death from her metastasizing cancer, said the following to me:

> You asked me what I think about my body. I've been proud of my body, because it was strong, because I could keep up with the children, because I was active. When they were little I was as active as they were and could do all the things they did, and even as they grew older I was still able to keep up with them. I was very proud of my body. I felt it was a good body, a very good body.
>
> And now, I wish I could shed it and get a new one. It's ruined everything I've had. Up until almost a year ago I was such a different person. You just can't imagine. And now, my body has let me down. And it's not just one or two parts, it's this complete exhaustion. I just have a terrible time trying to do anything. I'm just too tired. My body has really let me down.

We see here her regrets at what she had once been and her presentiment that she will get even worse, and we see her mourning her own decline and her eventual death. She said, in another session, that she was depressed and that part of her depression was related to her contemplation of what was happening to her, the further declines in vitality and energy that were apparently in store for her, and eventually her own death. She is, in a manner that is quite understandable, premourning herself. This realistic kind of premourning is psychologically sensible and is probably in the best interests of overall mental health. Self-mourning is an important aspect of the "death work" that each terminally ill person can do in the penultimate days of his life.

From the previous chapter the reader will remember the twenty-two-year-old man. A week or so before he died, he said this of himself:

> Now a perfectly good person with an awful lot to give is going to die. A young person is going to die. The death is going to be absolutely senseless.

Never mind that, in fact, his life and occupation might seem less than ennobled. One's achievements or strengths of character (as most of us might measure it) suddenly seem irrelevant to the dying person. Living persons mourn the recently dead; so do the dying mourn themselves as dead; both groups seem to follow the dictum: "Of the dead (say) nothing but good." *(De mortuis nil nisi bonum.)* Death is the omnipotent leveler—bringing the great of the world down to common ground—and it serves, in this leveling way, as the great equalizer.

That young, twenty-two-year-old person seems to say, I'm too good to die. Or, equally, he might say, I'm too young to die. But whatever is said, people uniformly seem to mourn a world that will be without them. And when you consider it sensibly, to mourn one's own death is a healthy psychological sign of proper self-respect.

The person who mourns himself has both fantasy and fact in mind: the comforting fantasy that he will be remembered as something special—"a perfectly good person with an awful lot to give"—and the omnipresent fact that we are all biodegradable matter.

The person who mourns most deeply for what might have been is that individual who knows the dying person best of all—knows intimately not only his talents but also his secret aspirations: the dying person himself. And that is why self-mourning can have a special poignant quality, all the more so because it often cannot be shared.

Self-mourning and denial can, and do, exist in the same dying person. There are moments of each; not necessarily alternating, not necessarily existing at the same moment, but present, in turn, during the days and weeks and months of the dying. The denial that occurs during self-mourning is in some ways similar to the hallucinated "assertions" (or re-creations) by the survivor of the recently dead person—hearing footsteps on the threshold or hearing breathing in the bed beside you. Those experiences are often a perfectly normal but nonetheless disturbing part of deep grief. In a way, they are themselves a denial that the death has taken place, but ordinarily they are no more pathological than was the dying person's denying that his own death was going to occur.

While self-mourning is the mourning of oneself before one dies, *premourning* is one's mourning of another person before that person dies. Premourning is made up of droplets of acute grief—the deep and overwhelming sense of loss and abandonment—while the loved person is still alive but obviously dying. Its psychological function would seem to be to inure the potential survivor, step by step—while there is still time—before the loved one's death, so that the event itself does not have the shocking effect of a sudden and unexpected catastrophe. Just as there are small deaths—departures, divorces, detachments—so are there also small griefs, rehearsals for the dreaded state to come.

Below are portions of a session with an older couple. After that first session I never saw the old gentleman again, but I continued to see the wife for another ten sessions before he died; and then I saw her for many sessions after that. In the very first session, she seemed to be just his shadow. It was difficult to say anything about her personality. But as she gradually disengaged from him (in order to protect her own sense of being), she seemed to emerge from the cocoon that her forty years of a delightful and admittedly overprotective marriage had been. From session to session, as she related the course of her premourning, she seemed to metamorphose into a mature and interesting adult, perhaps for the first time in her life.

Shneidman. This started for me when your daughter telephoned me.

Mr. T. Yes, well, I imagine that she explained things to you or at least her concern about us. And being three thousand miles away from us, she doesn't know what reaction we might have. Now, this cancer came on me quite suddenly and it's no doubt terminal and it isn't localized, as far as I know, and so I think that she's concerned about what our reaction might be. How we might take it as an individual or how we might react to the consequences involved in the outcome of it, is my understanding of it. Now, she calls us every evening and we talk to her, and I try to convince her that there is no cause for her concern. In other words, I don't think that she should be too concerned. It's a matter, as far as we're concerned, to live with and she has her own obligations, her business, and everything that she has to do, and I've tried to convince her that I didn't want her to get emotionally involved or really concerned about it. She says, Well, after all, I love my parents. I want to know what reactions you're having. This tumor has grown. And it was swollen up or something. And she says, I think that possibly you should have a biopsy. [And here he goes on for several minutes about medical details.] . . . But when they took this out under a local anesthetic, he took it up to the pathologist and he came back and said it's cancerous.

S. What went through your mind when he said that?

Mr. T. I kind of . . . he had kind of prepared me to expect it.

S. But nonetheless, what went through your mind?

Mr. T. No great emotion. I kind of expected it.

Mrs. T. Well, when they were wheeling him in, he looked up at me and he said, I have cancer. I didn't know anything about it until he looked up at me and said, I have cancer.

Mr. T. Dr. Jones told me and he said I'll talk to your wife later, he said you can tell her that it's cancerous.

S. And what was your reaction?

Mrs. T. I was just numb. I think that's what's the matter with me —I'm still numb.

S. Did you cry?

Mrs. T. No, no, I didn't cry. I didn't cry until just now.

Mr. T. This girl has lots of stamina—she's gone through a lot.

Mrs. T. And as I say, I refuse to think about anything further than tomorrow. Because—only God knows when it's time for my husband to go and that's what I'm going to believe. I don't believe anything else. And then I feel,

I've always done that, I feel when the time comes I don't know how I'm going to react to anything. I might start screaming. I might do anything. I don't know. How can a person tell? I really don't know. But I know I am emotional and I keep a lot of things embedded way down deep because there is no use in bringing them to the surface. Just accept life the way it is. Because I mean, you go through so much and you worry about so many things and then they've all turned out all right. And here I've made myself ill so many times, just worrying.

S. Really?

Mrs. T. Yes. And I've—I still worry to a point. I'm not strong . . . although our marriage—

S. You two have been married forty-some years?

Mr. T. Forty years.

Mrs. T. So I can almost sense . . . he doesn't have to tell me; I always know. . . . I would rather keep still—go out for a walk and get it out of my system, or go out and have a big chocolate sundae. Yes, one day I had two double-dip ice cream cones.

S. You must have been terribly upset.

Mrs. T. But when you know a man loves you the way he's always loved me and he knows how dearly I love him that we would never—could never possibly do anything that would hurt each other so deeply that we would think of sleeping in the other room or something. We never even had twin beds. For forty years we've slept in a full-size bed because we just don't want to be apart. And it's been that way. I don't show any emotion because I didn't want him to think I was so concerned that it would make him miserable. So I go out for my walk in the morning—and it's a furious walk, to get it out of my system, and then I come in and I'm nice and calm. We're not ordinary people, you know. He is the most unusual man you'll ever want to meet. And there isn't anyone who has ever met him that has ever thought otherwise.

Mr. T. I try to be very frank. I was with my mother and dad both when they died. I had no extreme emotion or anything. It didn't . . . bother me. I realize it was something that had to happen. . . . All in all, I think I've progressed to sixty-nine years old and something's bound to happen. It's going to happen. There is nothing in the world a person can do about it.

S. In what ways can I be of some help to either of you? What comes to your mind?

Mr. T. Just frankly speaking, I don't know of much you can do for me, because I'm inclined to believe that our thinking would probably go along the same channels—that maybe in preparation for it and the fact that it is inevitable, the fact that live to the best of your ability to the extent that I can. And I'm inclined to believe that her situation might be different. Now, as I say, I don't know that there's anything that you can do for me, but I think you can do something for my sweetheart, because I think—

Mrs. T. I don't know which way I'm going to go—I mean I really don't from day to day, because I kept the lid on it so long that I don't really know. I know that I'm going to need help. I feel that.

S. All right. I'll be happy to volunteer.

Mrs. T. I really do, because I don't want—I didn't ever want to see him suffer. If he begins to deteriorate, I think that's when I'll fall apart and I know it.

S. We'll watch it. You can both stay in touch with me as long as you want to. You can count on me as a resource.

Mrs. T. It's a comforting thought just to know that I will have someone to talk to. That helps already. Just knowing I will have someone to talk to.

S. I'll see you both soon.

He soon became too ill to do anything but receive outpatient treatments. But she wanted to continue to see me and, of course, she did. A few weeks later she reported that he had gone for a short walk in their neighborhood (where they had lived for years) and had become lost, disoriented, and could not remember his way back home. Some neighbors saw his plight, telephoned her and she went and brought him home. I silently surmised then that the cancer had metastasized to his brain. He had a rapid downhill course, becoming totally confused and disoriented, then went into coma and died, all within several weeks of that first session. The ways in which the wife wrestled with her premourning and, subsequently, with the loss and grief of his death are described below.

Only her opening remarks in each session are reproduced, so that we can see clearly the changes that occur over this few-month period.

Session Two (two weeks after the first session)

S. Now, unfortunately, some things have happened and not for the better since we met last.

Mrs. T. Because the day, if you recall . . . I said I couldn't cry? You know, I really couldn't feel anything. But now I'm getting the full realization of what's happened. Now I'm feeling all the emotions, like, for instance, when he rests in the afternoon I run in and I keep looking at him. At night I don't sleep —I keep looking, listening to see if he's breathing. And I'm developing fears, like, for instance, what do I do if I find him dead in his bed. What am I going to do. And all of a sudden I feel like I'm going to run out of the apartment. That's what goes through my head. It seems—I'm not in the right pattern with my life. For instance, I'm a very methodical person and orderly and I'm doing crazy things. I've never had a ticket or a citation in my life and I'm racing with everything—I got a ticket from a policeman. Never in my life, gone sixty years. Something's happening, my brain's not functioning. If I'm out for five minutes, if I open the door, I kind of tiptoe. . . . Isn't that ridiculous? It's all carpet, but I'm afraid of what? To see him. And this goes on every day now.

S. To see what?

Mrs. T. To see him dead. And then I begin to cry and then I have cried and cried and cried because I used to take a two-mile walk every morning with him. I made up my mind I was going to do it and see what happened. I cried all the way. And then I got such a feeling of depression that I was all alone. And that's the way it's got to be—that every day I would go out I would be alone.

S. You know . . . you're already partially alone.

Mrs. T. I know. I don't want him to know how I feel—that's why I came here alone. Yesterday he said, I wish I could go right now—then it wouldn't be so hard on you. Then I go off again and I feel—I can't cry every day and every night because I'm getting tired and I'm losing my vitality, which I don't want to happen. I want so to take care of him. And he said as long as you're with me and by my side, I'll be all right. He said, You wouldn't put me in a nursing home, would you? And I said, No. And I wouldn't, either. I hope you can understand I've never met anybody in my whole life that was ever . . . we've lived our lives together . . . I've always been his sweetheart.

Session Three (about two weeks later)

S. How are you feeling today?

Mrs. T. Well, I don't feel too bad today. I have my bad moments. For instance, each time I leave the house, and I go to the bank or go grocery shopping or need to go downstairs, why, I turn around and look at my husband . . . and he has such a longing look in his eyes: if he could only be with me. And that does it to me.

S. What do you do?

Mrs. T. Well, I get so built up and I feel energetic and I am going to get everything done and that look just . . .

S. Sort of takes the stuffing out of you.

Mrs. T. That's right. It does. And then I was thinking, you know, here I am worrying about me, how I am—and here this poor dear man sits here, he doesn't say a word, he just looks at me. And when I come back from being out, I think, O.K., dear, he's been alone. I started out fine this morning, like nothing in the world was wrong. I get up and I say, Why did I feel so good this morning?, you know, and I really did. And then after I get up and get dressed and did a few things that needed to be done, like get some money from the bank, cash a check and a few things, and I started out the door and I turned around, and he was looking so lonely. And I said, Maybe you'll be able to go with me next time. So I feel like he's kind of giving up because he doesn't say a word about trying anymore. And he only goes now from the bed to the chair, and the chair to the bed. I still cry every time I go to a place where we have been together. I've cut that out. I'm not going to those places. For instance, I used to go to the shopping center; it's indoors, everything's under one roof, and you know you can sit if you get tired. So we used to go up there every day and we would walk. And I hadn't been there for a long time. So I went up there Saturday morning to get him a pair of pajamas and I started walking, and you know, I just had to leave. Because I thought people would know—the tears—and I thought, I won't come back there for a long time until I feel up to it. And am I doing right by avoiding these places and—special places that we've gone and walked and done things—to avoid them?

Session Four (about a month later)

Mrs. T. My husband's back in the hospital.

S. Have you seen him today?

Mrs. T. Yes, and I told him I would be here until after eleven today. I had planned to come out here every day. I stay until after six-thirty. And that's a long day. I don't think I'm going to do that. I am literally exhausted—yesterday—when I get home. And I don't like to get tired. But I'll have you know that my husband's disposition is certainly changed since I've seen you. Oh, he is—he's so impatient. And I haven't been doing much crying. I've been angry! And frustrated, and I say how dare he talk to me so loud.

S. Does he actually holler at you?

Mrs. T. Yes, and he never did things like that. And he makes me feel incompetent and stupid. You know, if I've got to get something and I don't get it or do it right away, he'll grab it right out of my hand—he never did things like that to me. I could feel my stomach going like this because I can't say what I want to say. I can't say anything. I wouldn't say anything because I feel it's because of his condition. But even when he talked to our daughter on the phone, you should have heard him on the phone. And she said to her dad after he got through talking, she said, Put Mother back on the phone. So she said, What's the matter with him? And I said, Well, that's the way he's been, and I said, I'm glad he snapped at you so you won't think that I was a complaining mother. I can't figure it out. He scowls all the time. Of course, it doesn't mean . . . you don't think he's resentful of me?

S. Of what, dear?

Mrs. T. Of the energy that I have when he sees me and he's sitting in that chair all the time, and lying on the bed, and he's so helpless. Is it because . . . and I guess maybe of his condition probably. Do you think he feels less of a man because . . .

S. Of course, dear. Don't you think so?

Mrs. T. Well, I never thought of it along those lines. He's so furious when I open a door. He wants to do it. And I noticed—I've been noticing that too. And of course that breaks my heart.

S. Because his strengths are failing?

Mrs. T. Oh, he hasn't the strength of a kitten. . . .

S. And now he's been robbed of that and he's angry not only that you're seeing it but that he's seeing it.

Mrs. T. I never really thought of it in that light at all.

Session Five (two weeks later)

Mrs. T. I'm so nervous that I'm getting these violent headaches. Oh! My husband's personality is changing. Like for instance, I can still see him in the bedroom, he said, You make me so mad, and he was shaking his fist like that. If I didn't go along with everything he suggests, he is furious. And he's never a pleasant man anymore like he used to be. He screams at me.

S. What do you understand is going on?

Mrs. T. Well, all Sunday—he's coherent in a way—I said I'm going to call Susan and Robert. Those are our dearest friends. Those are the ones that say we're their adopted parents. And they are with us so much. He said who are they? And that was the first thing that he said on Sunday. Well, now he gets his words all mixed up—I mean they don't make sense. When he goes to describe something they're all the wrong adjectives. Do you know what I mean? They just don't make sense.

S. Can you give an example?

Mrs. T. He can't remember. He said to me, What kind of an illness do I have? What's wrong with me? And I said cancer. He said, I don't have cancer. You know I don't have cancer. And I said, Well, what did the doctor say? And I mean that's the voice he's talking in now.

S. That's a 180-degree turnabout from the first session we had. What do you think is going on with him?

Mrs. T. Well, I think something's affecting his brain. I think that those tumors must have something to do with it. I don't know how long I can go on like this. Because I feel sometimes that I'm going to stand there and just start screaming. I'm going to bat the wall down. Instead of that I go out of the house and I walk, especially if he's asleep. I just walk and walk! I cannot sit still. And I stay up until . . . weird hours. And wait until I'm so exhausted to go to sleep. And then if he wakes up he's yelling, Where are you? What are you doing? And if I want to leave him for a few minutes, he wants me to sit right next to him. I feel like someone who's trapped. . . .

Session Six (two weeks later)

Mrs. T. Yesterday he had the brain scan. They don't have the results ready yet. . . . He started using words that were just wrong words to describe things. And then he didn't know what town we were in. And he was saying streets where we lived when we were first married. That far back. And he'd say where is that and thinking it was in some other town. Oh, a friend of ours said they had a policy that they took out—they're retired people—for so much a year for a nursing home that both of them could go. And instead of him saying a nursing home, he said a concentration camp. Because you know he had been saying before that, Please don't put me in a nursing home because I won't be any trouble to you. . . . Do you think he feels something or is knowing something? And you know he also said, There's nothing wrong with my brain, I'm not crazy. Oh, he is such a proud man.

S. Yes.

Mrs. T. He wants to go out for that walk and he staggers even a little bit and if I go to hold him up he'll say, Don't hold me up, I can walk. But I don't know what to expect—what's frightening me is I don't know what to expect. I mean is he trying to . . . will this be a gradual thing or will he—something snap like that? There will be changes. That's what I'm frightened of. . . . It never occurred to me that he could have a tumor in his brain.

S. I'd like to know what happened to you yesterday. What was told to you and then what went through your mind when you heard that news?

Mrs. T. Well, I—I felt like I'd had a shock. I mean I stood and I—I couldn't comprehend it. The doctor said, The news is not very pleasant and I'm going to tell you, and I said, Tell me, because I don't like the slow approach. And he said, Your husband has a tumor on his brain and that's why he's been acting quite irrational, and I said, Oh, my goodness. And he said, Just stay calm. He said, I've called Dr. Shneidman and he told me to see you tomorrow. I didn't know there were people like you in the world that cared that much about other human beings. Because I've never had that and I've never needed it. Because with him, if anything was wrong he'd say, Oh, sweetheart, it's going to be all right. But now it's different. There's something wrong, but I don't have him to comfort me.

S. What was going through your head all this time?

Mrs. T. All this time I was thinking, This is . . . I was thinking, This is the way it's going to be now. I'm going to be alone. He will be gone and I will be running around like a chicken with its head off—like a crazy person. This is what's going through my head.

Session Seven (three weeks later)

Mrs. T. I had something happen to me that I wouldn't believe. I've heard people say it—you told me that I might feel this way at some time—but last night I came home, and I was feeling very low because my husband was pretty bad, so when I came home I looked at his hat and his cane and I just started crying. I thought, Well, this is the way it's got to be, and the next thing I knew, I could hear somebody screaming—and it was me. Like it was outside of me, it wasn't me at all. But I was crying and I could hear all this *aahh,* but I didn't know I was doing it. It was the strangest thing. And I really got frightened. It only happened for a little while and then I was just drained and I just felt ill.

S. What did you do then?

Mrs. T. I thought I can't lie here on my bed, because I'm thinking too much. I went in and turned on the music and then I called some friends—some very special friends I've had. So they both came over and he mixed a brandy and they stayed till two o'clock. They turned on the fireplace, they had the music on, they tucked me in. They wouldn't leave until they tucked me in. And then when they got home they called to see if I was all right. But then, strangely enough, I haven't cried since then. I feel different. I mean I walk in the apartment, I look at his hat and the cane and everything, and all of a sudden I don't feel—no emotion, I'm like I'm numb. Nothing seems to happen. What does that mean—what happened to me that I didn't even know that I was screaming? Like someone outside of myself or something.

S. The mind works in marvelous ways, in large part to protect itself. And in a way you are disengaging yourself from your husband.

Mrs. T. I think I've been trying so hard to learn to accept this. Because of what happened to me? Because of the way I am now?

S. Your mind has been rehearsing this.

Mrs. T. Because I thought it over in my mind so many times. I remember the day I put him in the hospital. That's the day it happened and you said—and I had to go home all by myself to my house, and that's when it happened. And now . . .

S. That's what it's going to be like.

Mrs. T. Well, I'm really going to need help, then.

S. Well, you'll get it. And you'll be able to live through it just as you're living through it now. And those peculiar things which you describe are normal for what is happening to you.

Mrs. T. Of course, I wondered what was really happening.

S. That's a normal reaction in a time of grief and you were experiencing what grief is like.

Mrs. T. Yes. Strangely enough, you said the word. I had that strange feeling like he was gone. Like he was dead. Like that came over me. And I thought, Well, this is the way it's going to be and I just wonder. Of course, I do have so many friends, but they can only do so much. They're not going to coddle me forever.

Session Eight (two weeks later)

S. Now we're meeting, and . . . it has happened, hasn't it?

Mrs. T. I keep telling myself that I won't cry.

S. Well, here are the Kleenex, and that's what they're here for.

Mrs. T. But you know, I feel numb?

S. Yes.

Mrs. T. And I can't drive my car. I just don't feel like it. I had someone drive me home yesterday. But physically I don't feel too great. How about that? I feel—my head is so mixed up with everything. I can't think clearly. . . . I feel like I'm in a trance; that's why I can't drive. But everything I do is just like I—like it's not me. I feel just like I'm walking around like a—you know, kind of like in a dream? I'm doing everything just automatically. I don't go to sleep until two or three in the morning. I just can't. And I stopped taking Valium because I don't want to depend on it. My body feels—you know that whole weak feeling from your head to your toes? That's just how I feel. Sort of like a rag doll.

S. Just depleted and wrung out.

Mrs. T. Absolutely. I feel if I could just go somewhere and just lie down and sleep for days and not open my eyes, that maybe I'd be all right. But I don't know if I would be or not. But I could just . . . the day I called you, I didn't know what was going to happen to me; that's why I thought if I could just talk to you. I thought maybe you could . . . I was reaching for something, I didn't know what it was, but as long as I knew you were on the phone I was all right. But I didn't know what was wrong with me, I didn't know if I was going to black out or I was going to scream or cry or I didn't know what was going to happen to me. But what did happen to me . . .

S. Tell me.

Mrs. T. I went in the closet and took all the clothes out and put them in a pile and I called my friend and I asked them if they'd please come over and take all those things. And then—that was only part of it. I got—I was carrying on hysterical and everything, but I was all right after that. And then when I opened the medicine cabinet and I saw all the stuff that he used, you know, that's when I felt that I couldn't stand it. Maybe that's why I'm so depleted. I usually wear my dark glasses because I don't know where I'm going to cry. I don't even go to the store. This friend of mine has come by and they'll bring me something, because they know I wouldn't eat otherwise. And then at night, that was terrible. But I—did I tell you that I did look at him in the casket?

S. Oh?

Mrs. T. Because I don't remember everything I said to you. I had no idea.

S. What went through you at those moments?

Mrs. T. I just wanted to . . . just die with him. They wouldn't let me look the next morning. I saw him the night before, you know? And Robert and Susan were with me and they were afraid I might maybe, you know, just act up. And they said, No, you saw him, you already said goodbye to him. The way they fixed him, he looked so handsome. He looked just like he did, you know. He really did. And I had to pick out the clothes, which I did. I was all right until a few days ago. All the time he was sick I could cope with it. But now that I know he's not here anymore, I keep thinking of how he looked that night at three o'clock in the morning. And how he kept choking all the time. That's what I've got to get out of my head, I know, and then I keep thinking of how nice he looked in the casket, then I'll stop, you know, crying. But all this stuff —my head, you know, seems to be a conglomeration. I can't clear it up. I can't. But as far as the—I just can't believe that he's not going to come home. To me in my head, it's like he's in the hospital. I want something that will snap me out of this trance that I'm in. Like the other night I went into the bathroom and I thought I could hear him whistle. Like he used to, you know? He used to whistle and say, What are you doing?

S. Did I tell you that you'll have that? That's an ordinary experience for a person in your condition.

Mrs. T. You told me that I would do that, didn't you?

S. People don't understand that that's absolutely normal.

Mrs. T. Oh, it is normal?

S. Oh, yes, the expected thing. You may hear his footsteps, you may hear his breathing in bed. You'll hear his whistle . . . and that's really not abnormal.

Mrs. T. It isn't?

S. No, it's more accurately called an extension of old habit patterns, an expectation.

Mrs. T. That's good to know. . . .

In that first session, I was undeniably impressed by the husband's force of character, and although I liked the wife, she did not impress me with her own ego strength. Her work in his life (and, I imagine, her image of herself) was simply to do his bidding, and to cater to his needs; in return, he would take care of her, totally. She did not seem to have a will of her own.

His illness—more accurately, his incapacity—and her insight

that she would soon be on her own changed all that rather dramatically. In the sessions excerpted above, we can see her grow almost from week to week, in terms of her self-understanding, her access to her own emotions, and in her capacities to move realistically in the world. She has the strength to call appropriately on others to help her or to do the tasks herself. In a canny and perspicacious way that cuts through her seeming psychological innocence, she senses quite accurately that he will die and that she will have to take care of herself. Instinctively she knows that she must not wait until he is actually dead before she begins this task of self-retraining. Rather, she starts on this most difficult self-assigned homework as soon as she receives the signals from her unconscious mind that her dependent-wife days are over and that she had better begin to premourn her beloved husband before she is actually faced with the real loss.

7

Mourning: Voices of the Bereaved

> "My boy, my own boy is among them. For God's sake—I beg, I conjure . . . you must, oh, you must, and you *shall* do this thing. . . . I will not go," said the stranger, "till you say *aye* to me."
>
> Herman Melville, *Moby Dick* (Chapter 128)

Mourning—the seemingly unquenchable and almost totally unsettling yearning for the return to life of the person who has recently and irretrievably disappeared—has many features in common with self-mourning and premourning. In a sense, the mourning for another after the death is an extension and a combination of one's mourning for oneself and one's mourning for another *before* death.

What are the sounds of mourning? They include wailing, weeping, beseeching and moaning; they include long outer silences and long inner dialogues; and they include, one hopes, helpful talk.

Working with bereaved persons by means of helpful talk can be called "postvention."[1] Prevention, intervention and postvention are roughly synonymous with the traditional mental health concepts of immunization, treatment and rehabilitation. Postvention consists of all those verbal and nonverbal activities that serve to reduce the dire aftereffects of a traumatic event in the lives of the survivors. Its purpose is to help survivors live longer, more productively and less stressfully than they would be likely to do otherwise.[2]

We know that recent investigations of widows by Colin Murray Parkes indicate that, independent of her age, a woman who has lost a husband recently is more likely to die (from a variety of causes) or to be physically ill than nonwidowed women.[3] The findings seem to imply that grief is itself a dire process and that there are subtle forces at work that can take a heavy toll unless they are treated and controlled.

These striking results had been known intuitively long before they were demonstrated empirically. The efforts of Erich Lindemann to aid survivors of particularly onerous deaths (which led to his formulations of crisis intervention) began with his treatment of the survivors of the tragic Boston Cocoanut Grove nightclub fire in 1942, in which almost 500 people died.[4] Lindemann's efforts in the forties are forerunners to the programs of "befriending" practiced by the Samaritans, a suicide prevention organization founded in the 1950s by the Reverend Chad Varah in Great Britain.[5]

The sudden death of a loved one can be viewed psychologically by the survivor as a disaster—those sudden, unexpected events, such as earthquakes and large-scale explosions, that cause a large number of deaths and have widespread effects. Martha Wolfenstein has described a "disaster syndrome": a "combination of emotional dullness, unresponsiveness to outer stimulation and inhibition of activity. The individual who has just undergone disaster is apt to suffer from at least a transitory sense of worthlessness; his usual capacity for self-love becomes impaired."[6] This psychological state can also be true of someone who has suddenly lost a loved one.

A similar psychological contraction is seen in the initial shock reaction to catastrophic news—death, failure, disclosure, disgrace, the keenest personal loss. Studies of a ship sinking[7] and the effects of a tornado[8] describe an initial psychic shock on the part of the survivors, followed by motor retardation, the flattening out of emotion, somnolence, amnesia and suggestibility. There is marked increase in dependency, with regressive behavior and traumatic loss of feelings of identity, and overall, a kind of "emotional anesthesia." There is an unhealthy docility, a cowed and subdued reaction. One is reminded of Lifton's description, in *Death in Life*, of the survivors of the atomic bomb dropped on Hiroshima:

> Very quickly—sometimes within minutes or even seconds—[people] began to undergo a process of "psychic closing off"; that is, they simply ceased to feel. They had a clear sense of what was happening around them, but their emotional reactions were unconsciously turned off. Others' immersion in larger responsibilities was accompanied by a greater form of closing off which might be termed "psychic numbing."[9]

Postventive efforts are not limited to this initial stage of shock, but are more often directed to the longer haul, the day-to-day living with grief over a year or more following the first shock of loss. Typically, postvention extends over months during that critical first year, and it shares many of the characteristics of psychotherapy: talk, ventilation, interpretation, reassurance, direction and even gentle confrontation. It provides an opportunity for the expression of usually guarded emotions, especially such negative emotional states as anger, shame and guilt. It puts a measure of stability into the grieving person's life.

Here are some verbatim excerpts from a set of two sessions —five years apart—with the parents of a young woman, their only daughter, who was murdered. The sessions took place one year and then six years after the precipitous death and one can clearly see the changes that have occurred.

Late one afternoon, a seventeen-year-old girl was stabbed to death by an apparent would-be rapist in the parking area of a government building. Within an hour, her parents were shattered by the news given to them by two rather young, well-meaning but inexperienced policemen. The parents' immediate reactions were incredulity, almost total shock, weeping disbelief, overwhelming grief and mounting rage, most of the anger directed toward the governmental agency where their daughter had been employed and where the murder had occurred.

A few days later, right after the funeral, they were in the office of a high official of the agency in whose parking lot the murder had taken place. He was attempting to tender his condolences, when the mother said in an anguished tone: "There is nothing you can do!" To which, with good presence of mind, he answered that while it was regrettably true that the girl could not be brought back to life, there was something that could be done. Whether he knew the term or not, it was postvention that he had in mind. He then brought them, personally, to my office.

The parents began to come for therapy, usually together, sometimes separately. The principal psychological feature of the sessions was the mother's anger. During the early sessions, she voiced her grief and vented her rage (often at me). My role was to represent the voice of reason: empathizing with their state, recognizing the legitimacy of their feelings. I felt that I was truly their friend, and believe they felt that I was theirs. I had asked that each of them see a physician for a physical examination. A few months after the brutal murder, the mother developed serious symptoms that required major surgery—from which she made a good recovery. The situation raises the intriguing (and unanswerable) question of whether or not that disorder would have manifested itself if she had not suffered the shock of her daughter's death. Within the year following the daughter's death, the mother had two additional extended hospitalizations. After the physical ailments were attended to, the parents were still in a state of low-level grief, and no doubt they always will be.

The father's mode of reaction was much more subdued. He

wept quietly, tried to calm her and seemed to adjust not so much by withdrawing but, almost literally, by "shrinking," which took the form of his aging rapidly—for example, his hair turned almost white within a year.

Here is an edited portion of a session exactly one year after the death:

Shneidman. Today is exactly a year, isn't it?

Mrs. Exactly. And it was just about this time when she was killed.

S. Can you say something about what this last year has been like?

Mrs. Well, at first the grief was extremely intense. It was actually a physical pain. For a couple of months I went around and it hurt. It actually hurt, in here. And I felt I was carrying the world on my shoulders and inside of me.

S. When you say that it hurt in here, are you pointing to where you had your chest surgery this past year?

Mrs. No, not really. It just hurt, that's all.

Mr. I don't think the pain was physical. It was more mental.

Mrs. No, it wasn't. I mean it hurt physically. But it was a mental pain.

Mr. There are times when the pain is still there. It's hard to describe it. It's just there. A feeling of pain. I guess it's part of sorrow.

S. A kind of unbearable anguish?

Mrs. Yes. We had a very bad day yesterday, and much more so today.

S. Yes, of course.

Mrs. You can't just cut off seventeen years in one day. It was like losing an arm or a leg or something. Or a head, because you can do without an arm, and you learn to do, in a way, to do without a daughter. It sounds so trite when you say it that way.

Mr. I think one of the things that has happened in the past year is that, as far as I'm concerned, I don't think I've discussed it too much but I'm more capable of facing the situation, of thinking about it. I used to try to put it out of my mind. For a while there, the hardest thing I had to do was look at her picture.

S. Do you still have it displayed in your house?

Mr. We have one in our bedroom on our bureau. It stays there all the time, but, uh, I don't get a shock anymore when I look at her picture.

S. Your reactions over the past year have been very different, because you are, in fact, very different people.

Mrs. I still turn around to look when I see the hair bobbing up and down and I still turn to look, and then I realize how stupid it is. I still look to see if it's her. It's always in the back of my mind anyway.

S. It's always there, ready to pop up.

Mrs. I mean you've been very good for us, because there was someone we could talk to. And someone that could show —in a way, take a different viewpoint. How can we see beyond our noses when we're so grief-stricken?

Mr. That's what I was trying to bring out a while ago, that is what you've helped us—me—in facing the truth.

S. How was that done?

Mr. I don't know, just the fact that I was discussing rather freely, maybe.

Mrs. And we thought we could tell you anything and you wouldn't be angry or—I don't know exactly how to say it, but I always felt we could talk to you and we could tell you exactly what we thought and not face any recriminations or anything like that.

S. Speaking of anger and recriminations, there was a time when you were terribly angry.

Mrs. Yes.

S. What's happened to that anger?

Mrs. It's dissipated. At first, in the beginning, I was ready to kill everybody and anybody.

S. Including me.

Mrs. Including you, because you represented the institution to us.

Mr. Not really.

Mrs. Yes, in a way he did, because I blamed the institution for her death. I still feel that somebody here helped, did his part in getting her killed, by turning out the lights, by not patrolling, by not doing something—a sin of omission is just as big as a sin of commission.

Mr. I don't think that any one individual is responsible for that.

Mrs. Well, he did it.

S. A kind of negligence?

Mrs. Yes. That's what I mean by a sin of omission. Let's say this—the parking lot was not safe.

S. So there are still certainly reservoirs of anger and blame.

Mrs. At the time I wanted the man caught and killed.

S. The actual murderer?

Mrs. The murderer. Now I would just like him stopped, but I don't want him killed. Will that bring her back? People were afraid of us, they were afraid to talk to us.

Mr. Some still are.

Mrs. Some of them still are, because they didn't know what to say. It was a difficult thing, it's a difficult thing for most people to find words of sympathy. What do you tell parents whose daughter is killed like that? Another thing that in a way you taught me is to take one day at a time.

S. How did I teach you that?

Mrs. I don't know how, but that's what I've been doing, taking one day at a time.

S. Today you seem like you're almost back six months ago, compared to our last visit of a couple weeks ago, in terms of the intensity of your feelings and the intensity of your anger. I haven't seen it at this intensity for some months; and it may be that this occasion, the anniversary, reintensifies it. Did our sessions play any role in controlling those feelings? Did they put them in some kind of perspective?

Mrs. Yes, you were able to really show us, in a proper perspective. That's one of the things you did, you were always the one to look at things in a straight manner. How could we, when we're so prejudiced about everything—I mean about what happened to her. We're so close to the forest, we can't see the trees.

Mr. I think you've also managed to curtail her anger in general to a certain extent, because she was mad at the whole world at the time—any reason. She'd get very mad.

S. Have there been some changes, really, in sort of your general character?

Mrs. I think so. I've been probably a little bit more tolerant.

S. To what do you attribute that?

Mrs. The whole thing—not just the death, but to our meetings. We get more used to it. I suppose we will become more resigned to it, that she isn't here, she won't come back, and that going to the cemetery won't hurt so much. But I try not to make this a special day because what's to celebrate? But it is, in a way, a special day.

S. It is an occasion to memorialize.

Mrs. It was sad to come home last night and find that he was crying. He had said prayers for her last night.

Mr. It was just a defense mechanism. I was crying to keep you from crying, so you would feel sorry for me for a change.

Mrs. I suppose in a way it made me less intolerant of other people. But what a price to have to pay. What a pity. All those years. There is something so final now. I used to feel that there was continuity. That she would have children, and in a way live on. He is the last male of his line. The last one of his family.

Mr. It's the end of the name anyway.

S. There is a sense of being cut off from the future, isn't there?

Mrs. Cut off. You have children and they will eventually marry and have children of their own and you will have grandchildren and in a way part of you will live on forever.

S. It is true. I have thought about that.

Mr. I imagine there is going to be a lot of hurt when we have to attend weddings or births.

Mrs. Somehow it is very hard to think that when you die, that's the end. But it's not as bad as when I used to be afraid of death. I am no longer afraid of death, personally. It's no longer such a terrible thing. It was terrible, I suppose, because it was unknown. Another time I would have been afraid when I went into the hospital. I was so unafraid that I believed the doctor when he told me before the operation that it wasn't going to hurt. How naïve can you be? I wanted to believe it. I'm sure that I could not have gone through this past year without him [her husband].

S. I think you have clung to each other in a marvelous way.

Mr. Except for one time when she almost walked out on me.

Mrs. That's different. That didn't count. To get through the impossible days and even longer nights. I still dream of her and when I would dream of her, I dream of her the way she was.

S. What kind of dreams do you have about her?

Mrs. They go back in time when she was alive and all the time I know she's dead. We're talking and doing just the things that we used to do. And talking about the same problems that we had before and she was just like she truly was. I don't see her through a rosy glow and all the time I know that she is dead. At the time I am dreaming, in a way I know I am dreaming, as I know that she is dead. Subconsciously I know that she is dead and I always say that I am glad that I can still see her as she was and not because we were as we were. We were not perfect and she was not perfect. Of course, no one will ever bring up any of her faults now.

S. No. One does not speak ill of the dead.

Mrs. No. Everybody when they do talk about her glosses over any of her faults. No one wants to talk about them. I don't know of anyone who has voluntarily brought up her name but you.

S. But there is a certain essence that remains.

Mrs. Yes, from far, far away.

S. Maybe that's how you stay in people's memories. She certainly still lives in that sense.

Mrs. She still lives as long as we live.

S. Yes, and some others.

Mrs. That's true, but you know that there is continuity, generally speaking, in a family. Right now, looking back, I see what a terrible waste the whole thing was. What a pity to have to die so young.

Mr. In one of the cabinets in our house we have the stupidest things there. We have an ashtray that she made for us. A thing of clay. A pencil holder.

S. It is understandable that you would keep those.

Mrs. Because they mean something to us. She had a way of looking through a lot of our friends. Our friends seem so much older.

S. Do you feel older?

Mr. Very much. We were discussing this not too long ago and we both felt we had missed out on middle age—that we went from youth to old people.

S. Really. You feel that way?

Mrs. Most of the time. I feel so old, and I caught myself talking to my brother and I said, When we were young, and he said, Look, you are talking about only a couple of years ago.

S. Well, what we need to do is bring back the sense of youthful middle age.

Mrs. I don't think that will ever come back. I always felt inside that I was about nineteen or twenty. And now I feel sixty years old. I feel so old.

S. I remember a sharp interchange between you and me. It was very soon after her death and you said in effect there was nothing that could be done. Obviously, I didn't believe that. I felt that something could be done.

Mrs. That's what I mean when I said we could talk to you and tell you anything and not worry about recriminations.

You taught us a great deal, and even when you expressed disapproval.

Mr. There were times when I actually felt that you were trying to make her mad at you.

S. I never did that. I didn't need to.

Mrs. I always felt that you like me. I remember the look on your face when I showed you her picture. I will never forget it.

S. I can't describe what went through me.

Mrs. You showed it. It was like hitting you and you absolutely recoiled as though I had hit you. I have her picture still.

Mr. What a time for my nose to be running.

S. What do you think about our next meeting? When do you think it ought to be?

Mrs. I miss you when I don't see you.

S. How often do you think we ought to meet now?

Mr. They've been about a month apart.

Mrs. I would hate to think about our meetings finishing, ending.

S. Well, we don't have to worry about that today. Let's think about meeting four weeks from today.

Mrs. Yes.

Mr. Yes.

S. Let's do it.

Clearly, after one year, some healing had occurred; clearly, many deep scars remained. As in any therapeutic exchange, the importance of a caring interpersonal relationship cannot be overstated. The willingness to help, the establishing of good rapport, the effecting of positive transference (and countertransference), are really the bedrock. The second point relates specifically to mourning and grief: It becomes evident from my work with this couple and other bereaved persons that the crisis-intervention model (of three months or six sessions) on which a sizable segment of current work with survivor victims is based simply is not in harmony with the way that most people do their grieving. I would not wish to give some other time period as though it were fixed or magical, but my general impression is that the acute stage of mourning lasts at least around one year; not the state of shock or numbness that sometimes immediately follows the loss, but rather the ability to function in the world without biting distress, yet with intervals of controllable tears, and an ache so severe that one cannot open one's eyes to see any beauty in the world.

Five years later—six years after the murder—they spoke as follows:

Shneidman. It's the anniversary again.

Mrs. It's been six years.

S. Please bring me up to date. Tell me how you are and what you're doing.

Mrs. Oh, I've just started a new job; it's in a real estate company. It seems very interesting. You know I didn't work for some time.

Mr. We've moved again, moved our apartment.

S. Isn't that the third move in the last six years?

Mrs. Well, we were in a pretty isolated place. I don't drive and we lived in a place for a while that was in the middle of nowhere.

S. You look absolutely radiant. Do you have a new hair style? You're wearing eye make-up; I've never seen that before on you.

Mrs. Well, I'm working.

S. Your eyes are bright. Do you feel as well as you look?

Mrs. No, not really; it's been a rough couple of weeks. It's a terrible time of year particularly. Her birthday would have been on the tenth.

S. Are anniversaries like that, birthdays and other anniversaries?

Mrs. Birthdays seem to be the hardest for me all the time.

S. What happened on her birthday this year?

Mrs. I went to work, but we went to the cemetery the Sunday before. We don't go as often as we did.

Mr. We used to go about once a month. In the past year I think it's been decreasing.

S. Did you really? So it's a part of your lives.

Mr. It's something I just feel that I want to do. Put some fresh flowers on her grave.

Mrs. We go to all the graves; all four are close together—my mother and father, my sister and hers.

Mr. There are two more plots available to us, that belong to us.

S. How often do you visit the cemetery?

Mr. We haven't done that in a long time. This past year we've been there about three times. It's just when we get an urge we go.

S. What are your feelings there?

Mr. They vary. There are times when I feel like crying and there are times when there's no emotion in me. The grave, the name, reminds me of things.

Mrs. It's always a shock to me to return there. She would have been twenty-three years old.

S. I'm sure you do that arithmetic all the time.

Mr. Well, all your life.

Mrs. Yeah, I'm afraid I will. . . . Our niece is married. She's living in Denver.

S. That marriage was a painful episode for you, wasn't it?

Mrs. Yes, that was very difficult. Other children aren't always difficult anymore. I have a number of friends who have daughters who are very kind to me.

S. Will your niece's having a baby be an occasion of some trauma for you, some distress?

Mrs. It might be; I don't know. When people you know show their grandchildren and stuff like that.

S. Yes.

Mr. Something else that we've noticed—they—when people, friends, are discussing family and children, there always seems to be a sort of tension where they stop the conversation. Even when we meet strangers that friends of ours have already introduced to us, that they never ask about our children. I think that somebody's warning them all about us.

S. Yes. And you're acutely sensitive to this.

Mrs. Of course.

Mr. I don't know if we're acutely sensitive, but we notice it anyway.

Mrs. Yes, we are very supersensitive on that point really.

Mr. Although I've found a lot of people that took a lot of interest years ago have forgotten all about it. They seem to be shocked all over again when the subject comes up. I don't mean real close friends, but acquaintances, people that I work with, I worked with for the past eight or ten years. People don't care to remember things like that, I guess.

Mrs. It's yesterday's news.

S. What seems to have helped you most?

Mrs. What's helped me most is knowing that my husband is there.

S. Having each other?

Mrs. Yes.

Mr. I think we've grown closer together than we ever have before.

Mrs. I know that the pain is not as intense as it was previously.

Mr. I think that time has more to do with it than anything else.

Mrs. At times—at times it gets very bad and at times it's much better. As I say, it doesn't fill my mind all the time. But suddenly sometimes I happen to see a blond girl or someone will walk or say something the way she did and all of a sudden everything comes right back again. I know she would be twenty-three, but I can't imagine that, I don't know what her life would have been.

Mr. She comes up in conversation quite often, but she's not a main topic of it.

Mrs. We have these friends who are very close because I think that's one of the ties it—thing that ties us; also they like to play cards with us.

S. I take it there's laughter in your life now that you can play cards and have a drink and laugh and talk.

Mrs. Oh, yes. We've never really gone on a trip alone, we've always had friends along.

Mr. Well, on that type of trip.

Mrs. It's peculiar; I have always had trouble sleeping, especially since she died, but on the ship I sleep. I think it's the rocking, that and nobody can get to me when I'm on a ship.

S. What does the future look like? How do you see yourselves, say a few years from now? Will you be even more mellow?

Mr. I think so. We're looking forward to the day when we can retire and really concentrate on traveling.

S. How nice.

Mrs. That sounds a lot better than it is.

Mr. It's still a long way off.

Mrs. I think of you often.

S. You do?

Mrs. Yes.

S. What do you think about when you think about me?

Mrs. Well, I think about—I think what on earth—I often think what we would have done if we didn't have you as a—I don't think we could have done it without you.

S. At one time you said, "We would have done it, but perhaps not as well."

Mrs. I was going to say not as easily, but it wasn't easy.

S. Yes.

Mrs. I don't know, it would have been very, very much more difficult.

S. You must have some ambivalent feelings toward me. How do you feel about me?

Mrs. Oh, well, I suppose like a father, more like that. I always felt that I could tell you the truth. You can't always tell people the truth.

S. Do you still see me as part of the institution?

Mrs. I don't think I see beyond you as a person. I never associated you with the institution. It's always been a personal thing to me.

S. At the very beginning you said, I think, that I was a minion of the institution, but that dropped away, I guess.

Mrs. It has never been—I mean this is where you see people. That's why we came here. But you've never been associated with the institution. I never had—perhaps at the very beginning, but you've never been an adversary. You've always been a friend. If you were to ask my feelings, I would say that I loved you.

S. I'm very moved by that. It's a rare occasion in life to feel that you can help a person in a really troubling situation. I was just enormously moved by that terrible tragedy and I wanted to do anything I could. And I don't have to say that now I'm very fond of both of you.

Mrs. I know that. I mean this to me is a very special thing. I mean this was a spontaneous thing. You know when I saw you, the first time I saw you, you were walking, we were walking one way down the hall and you were walking the other way and I knew who you were and I knew right away that we would have, I mean that we could communicate. You know, you can never really tell people all the truth all the time. I wonder sometimes if you had not had children; no, I don't think so. Are you still writing?

S. Yes, right in the middle of it.

Mrs. I've seen your name in the paper a couple of times and I go, whew, that's my therapist. It was totally by accident that we saw it and there you were.

S. All right, dear friends. Can I walk you out to your car?

Mrs. Surely. Are you going out?

S. I'll just walk you to your car.

One of the main things we see from these sessions is that the burden of a sudden, unexpected death—whether natural, accidental, suicidal or homicidal—is onerous enough, but murder (and suicide) impose a special and heavy burden on the survivor. That load is made up of at least four weighty components: the stigma of murder or suicide; the special unnerving effect of having a loved one murdered, raising the specter that you yourself might suffer a similar fate; the disturbing images of blood and violence produced in the mind; and the obsession of the survivor with the whos, the whys, the whats and the ifs. Those obsessions crowd the mind for years. They fill the thoughts in the day and the dreams in the night. That can be the enduring curse of a sudden, unexpected, violent and stigmatizing death; it doesn't go away as easily as what we might call a normal, expected death of a loved one.

How true is the statement that time heals all wounds? What has happened in the half-dozen years after the murder; what changes have occurred between the session one year after and the session six years after the death of these parents' daughter? Based on what I have seen in this and other cases (and what I know of human nature), the following appears to be true.

In the first year, there has been some dissipation of the acute anger, especially the somewhat irrational anger toward the institution where the murder occurred, and certainly a reduction in the hostile feelings toward the therapist, who was initially viewed by the parents as being identified with the "murdering" institution. In fact, there has been a sharp increase in the warm feelings toward the therapist, reflecting the emergence of positive transference feelings. The irrational hostility has all but disappeared; in its stead is a somewhat exaggerated affection, a viewing of the therapist as benign, paternal and protective.

In the interval between the first and the sixth year there was either the danger of a complete splitting apart and possible divorce—based on mutual irrational accusations relating to the daughter's death as well as their different ways of handling stress—or the possibility of a stronger growing together and a firmer bonding between them, cemented by their mutual grief. In this case, the latter occurred.

There has been a general mellowing, some obvious premature aging and a pervasive low-grade sadness. Especially in this case where the victim was an only child, the expected ties to future generations through grandchildren (and their children, etc.) were severed, and the scope of their lives, in this psychobiological sense, understandably truncated. A significant part of their "future" was irretrievably denied to them.

On the other hand, there have been some (typical) restorative behaviors—in the form of travel, work, social interaction with friends. Superficial observation might make it seem that the recovery is quite complete, but closer scrutiny easily reveals those tender scars that will remain forever.

Mourning is one of the most profound human experiences that it is possible to have. Even if it is not possible for an individual to conceptualize his own death, it remains undeniably true that a person can actually experience the death of another—and to feel the sense of emptiness, loss, fear and bewilderment.

Grief and mourning can have the effect of reducing a well-functioning child or adult to a howling and bereft person, to an almost animal-like creature. But even at those very same moments, the grief-stricken person displays what is also the most human-like of all his characteristics: the need and capacity for social, personal and loving relationships and bonds. The deep capacity to weep for the loss of a loved one and to continue to treasure the memory of that loss is one of our noblest human traits.

Part Four

Concluding Thoughts

8

Toward a Better Death

> I joy that Death is this Democrat; and hopeless of all other real and permanent democracies, still hug the thought that though in life some heads are crowned with gold, and some bound round with thorns, yet chisel them how they will, head-stones are all alike.
>
> Herman Melville, *Pierre* (Book XX)

Some of the kinds of death described in this book are unusual. It is extremely unlikely that many of us will be executed; relatively few of us will commit suicide. However, a sizable number of the readers of this book may be touched by a life-threatening illness—either in their own lives or in the lives of their loved ones. I began this book by saying that I hoped to provide a rutter for death—that is, to share a number of personal documents that might light the way and give the reader some ideas of what to avoid in life's journey, especially toward the end of it (at whatever age), and some ideas of what choices might be made.

By the use of others' personal documents I have tried to give the twin topics of death and dying a sense of immediacy. I have attempted to make them dramatic for the reader and to show a variety of possible scenarios for his or her own death.

There is no single best kind of death. A good death—very close to Avery Weisman's notion of "an appropriate death"[1]—synchronizes with your own particular needs and is tailor-made so that it is meaningful for you. A good death for you is one in which the "hand" of your way of dying slips easily into the "glove" of your death. A good death meets your own needs, within the context of the wishes and needs of your loved ones and your own social milieu. It is "ego-syntonic"—it fits you. The important point is that even if you cannot choose the manner of your dying, you can choose to think about the way in which you will die and perhaps change it a little bit so that it is more acceptable to you and to your loved ones.

One can die from a life-threatening illness over a period of time in a variety of ways. One can rage into the night (as the poet Dylan Thomas would have it); go like a good child to bed; view the entire process as a new experience as though one were an interested observer—after all, you have never died before; be fearful and quake in uncontrollable ways that exasperate one; be regretful and rueful, almost nostalgic; be contemplative and somewhat resigned. There is sweet surrender ("Come sweet death") and resignation, and there is terrorized capitulation; there is the fight for autonomy and control or the passive and dependent handing of one's body over to the doctors and technicians; there is optimism that is discriminating and optimism that is denial; and there is et cetera, *und so weiter,* and so on. In other words, a large number of styles to accommodate a vast number of different kinds of people.

Here are the opening paragraphs of a dying memoir written by a young woman, just turning twenty. She is not professionally established or highly schooled. She has been married for a few years and has a year-old baby daughter. She also has osteosarcoma, a life-threatening cancer of the bone. These passages by Lyn Helton were first published a few months after she died. They are entitled "Soon There Will Be No More Me."[2]

> Dying is beautiful—even the first time around, at the ripe old age of 20. It's not easy most of the time, but there's a real beauty to be found in knowing that your end is going to catch up with you faster than you had expected, and that you have to get all your loving and laughing and crying done as soon as you can. . . .
>
> I am going to try my damnedest to get this book done. . . .
>
> I have so many things to write about, so many things to pour out to someone who will listen. But it's hard to write about things that hurt, and things that need to be thought out privately, when you know someone else will be reading them.
>
> In the beginning I always tried to keep comforting thoughts flowing in my mind, things like "don't worry, it's a wrong diagnosis" or "surely they have a cure for this somewhere!"
>
> But as I slowly realized the seriousness of having cancer, my attitude changed. I got scared. Sometimes I couldn't even sleep at night. I'd sit up, wrapped in a blanket, in my old green rocker until I'd be sick to my stomach—and I'd vomit alone, in the darkness, while my husband and baby slept, and I'd just be scared.
>
> What's it like to die? If someone would just tell me maybe I'd feel better.

There are several points to be noted in those poignant passages. There is the wish for some completeness, closure, accomplishment: to finish her book, to leave a mark, a something after she is gone, to have some lien on her husband and especially her infant daughter, to live on in some however ephemeral ways beyond her own life. I have called this notion the post-self, and I mean by it the hunger—"O my hunger," said the poet Anne Sexton—of the dying person not to be totally expunged from the minds and hearts of loved ones, not to be completely forgotten too soon.

We are also haunted by this young woman's words ". . . there's a real beauty to be found in knowing that your end is going to catch up with you faster than you had expected." Jean Cocteau, the great contemporary French poet and author, said, "The beauty of failure is the only lasting beauty. Who does not understand failure is lost." Elaborating on this theme (in the final paragraph of his book *Cancer: The Wayward Cell*), Dr. Victor Richards, a cancer specialist, has these reflections about the failure of death:

> [One who does not understand failure] is lost to the hope and the deepening of experience that failure offers. In the elation of success, when we ride the crest of the wave, our sense of power blinds us. Success is intoxicating, and the intoxication is authentic, as are all our experiences. But success is not the whole. In the hollow of the wave, in failure and in the approach to death, we can experience a humble power, and the knowledge of peace. Physicians and families care best for the dying patient by helping to make death an inevitable but positive experience, from which none of us is spared.[3]

Cocteau and Richards would seem to hold a view that implies that failure, in itself, has some peculiar mystical, lofty and cleansing quality; that under many circumstances, failure (read: the dying process) is good for the soul, refining, elevating, strengthening. Perhaps. And perhaps not. Certainly there is another side to it. That opposite view would begin by asking: Who needs it?

To laud failure, to list the merits of it, is, in my mind, a specious rationalization. Cocteau's clever turn of phrase aside, is it true that a person who has not experienced failure is really lost? But the question itself is moot and hollow, because we know that it is simply not possible to live to nursery school age without experiencing a number of keenly felt rejections and defeats. So, under Cocteau's dictum, no one need fear being lost. But should we seek out failure—which, we need to remind ourselves immediately, is a different question from should we seek out death?

The English psychiatrist John Hinton writes in a vein somewhat different from the American Richards. He presents the following view:

> It is those who are discontented with themselves, dissatisfied with the routine of their lives and frequently exhausted by their own emotional conflicts, that think of the peace that death might bring. The apparent acceptance of death is often spurious, however. Although they may often feel that death's ease would be welcome, it would be a peace at the price of *failure.* Their wish for surcease from the struggle, which is based on a desire for greater fulfillment in life, could not be answered by the *fiasco* of dying. Although the rest from turmoil might be welcome, death would leave so much undone, so many ambitions unfulfilled. Only if all hopes are surrendered, will despair make death and failure acceptable. [Italics added.][4]

Jory Graham is a journalist who has cancer and who has written about it in a biweekly column in a Chicago newspaper. She has thought about the question of failure:

> If our lives are to have any significance, it's up to us [the people with cancer] to turn our tragedies [failures] into triumphs of sorts. And the way to achieve this is by somehow managing to reach out to those who are trying to share our burden with us.[5]

Graham has given three important insights in this short excerpt: First, when one is in dire straits, often the best that one can hope for is some "triumphs of sorts"; not the most overwhelming triumphs, but some little successes that will have to do. Second, that in order to achieve even this triumph, one must "somehow" manage to reach out, although reaching out (when one is threatened by cancer and in terror and pain) is precisely what is difficult. And finally, that while triumphs can be shared, for the dying person, pain and failure are private and unsharable.

There is no best way to die (of cancer or of anything else). In my own search for some talismanic rule of thumb, I have found nothing more comforting than the wisdom of my beloved mentor and friend Dr. Henry A. Murray. He speaks of *"a forthright willing of obligatory."*[6] What I understand this to mean (in relation to death and dying) is that there is a great difference between an obligation and an obligatory. To have to visit one's commanding officer's home on a certain ceremonial occasion is an obligation; dying is an obligatory—there is *no* choice. The key to willing the obligatory is to participate in one's own life, including one's pain and dying, with as much *grace* (elegance, poise, self-possession, pride, purpose, good manners, good cheer) as one can.

Baldassare Castiglione, the sixteenth-century Italian diplomat and man of letters, in his famous *Book of the Courtier (Il Cortegiano),*[7] has given us, across the centuries, a rutter for grace. It is "that seasoning without which all the other properties and good qualities would be of little worth . . . avoiding affectation in every way possible as though it were some very rough and dangerous reef. . . . concealing all art and making whatever is done and said appear to be without effort and almost without any thought about it. Much grace comes of this: because everyone knows the difficulty of things that are rare and well done"—like dying with grace, especially when one is frightened and in pain.

And what of the pain of dying? By and large, so far as I can see, there is little or no actual pain in dying. Granted that there can be great suffering in disease, but dying is the end of disease and thus the end of misery. (There is, of course, pain in being tortured or beaten to death, but for most of us, these are not likely.) The principal pain in dying lies in the deep fear of the supposed pain of death. This is so because "death" has erroneously been given a "life of its own," as though it were an experience, or a state of being, or a transition to some horrendous mythological lower place. Nowadays, we can view dying more realistically as that relatively short period in which the individual reverts to being an essentially biological organism and withdraws (often in coma) to nurture itself in its last moments. In the gut-level wisdom of the body, these last moments are pain-free, governed by a still active brain that is inured to almost everything but its own last few, fragmented feelings, and bent on trying to protect itself as well as possible from the very pain that it previously might have feared.

To will the obligatory in relation to death is to fall in line with the major immutable cycles of nature, especially human nature, and to understand that (whether or not there is a purpose or meaning to life) no one, absolutely no one, escapes being finite and mortal. And knowing this, then to accept it, to will it, and not to be in an unnecessary state of angst or rebellion or terror over it.

There are connections between the idea of willing the obligatory and Ernest Hemingway's definition of courage as "grace under pressure." Willing the obligatory is not merely a passive act of capitulation to the inevitable, but rather a complicated act of perception, imagination, will and behavior, in which you can seize the opportunity to use what is most heroic and sterling within yourself and do life's most difficult task as well as possible.

It is logical here to ask about the place of religion and faith. In the chapter on enforced execution, we saw, in the letters of the condemned, the use of the imagery of the tree as a symbol of life. Here is another such example, this one relating to faith, written in a Nazi prison by a German pastor to his wife.

> Once again the chestnut tree is preaching a sermon to me. Its bare black branches reach out to me so promisingly bearing the small brown buds for next spring. I can see them close to the window and also in the top branches. They are already there even when the yellow falling foliage was still hiding them. Should we be so thankless and of so little faith that we deliberately overlook among the falling, withered leaves . . . the buds that here cling tenaciously to trunk and branches? . . . Let us go on holding only ever more firmly and unequivocally to faith, live by it and act by it, because faith alone represents the victory over the prison of this world and its lethal power.[8]

That superb passage can serve as a spiritual Rorschach blot; each of us can project upon it whatever we wish to define as the cornerstone of our faith: Jesus, Jehovah, Confucius, Mohammed, Buddha, Krishna, Zeus or faith in our own integrity as a finite human being. It is not that the person who eschews organized religion is bereft; it is that the person who lacks some stabilizing beliefs—even (or especially) in one's self—is lost.

What you have to fight is hopelessness—even under torment, despite whatever calamities, however bleak the outlook. Hope is the keystone; faith and courage-with-pride are the two pillars on which it rests. These words—faith, courage, pride, hope—are easy to misinterpret. Each has to carry a great deal of weight.

What is the place of philosophy and belief? Take the question, posed by philosopher Stephen Pepper: "Can a philosophy make one philosophical?"[9]—that is, can one's thoughts make one calmer about dying?

Pepper asserted that in all of man's history, there have been just a few comprehensive and adequate philosophies, which he called "world hypotheses." Continuing, he commented as follows:

> An explicit philosophy is a guide greatly superior to a purely institutionalized ideology or creed. For even when not inadequate, the latter is rigid and dogmatic, whereas the former may be flexible and open to revision.[10]

As a clinical thanatologist, I would go further and say that what seems to be important is not so much the content of any philosophy of life, religion or creed, as how firmly, easily and comfortably that belief is held.

When one is dying, the most important criterion of the usefulness of a belief system or creed is not its truth value but the internal comfort which that belief system gives to that person. This would seem to be so whether the person is creedishly devout, quietly agnostic or querulously atheistic, as long as that person has (what may appear from someone else's view) the courage of his own confusions. In this sense, it is rather similar to your being comfortably in love with someone. The rational question: "What do you see in *that* person?" is not as important as your being able tranquilly (on whatever rational or emotional or unconscious grounds) to answer: "I like that person's company; it comforts me." If one can say with Martin Luther—but with a multiplicity of meanings—*Ich kann nichts anders* (I can do no other), then you can be true to yourself and die as well as one can.

Some final personal words: It has not been humanly possible to work with suicidal and dying persons as I have done—or to have written this book—without having intermittent thoughts about my own death. I see now that this book is my own personal document of death. It is a diary I need not write, a public mourning I need not make, a sharing of feelings I need not disguise, and most profoundly for me, it is—as is every one of my prolonged contacts with a dying person—a painful but I hope therapeutic rehearsal for my own death.

What, then, does it mean to die? I need a new word, somewhere between the words "fear" and "dread." Perhaps the word "anguish" comes closest. What anguishes me the most is the idea of naughtment: to abandon my loved ones, to disappear as though I had never been, to be "oblivionated." I know that will occur, but nonetheless I have a deep investment in my "post-self," my reputation or memory-in-the-minds-of-others, especially my children and their children and then their children (whom I shall never know). I distinguish between my cessation—the final stopping of my active consciousness, which I equate totally with "my life" ("No mind, no self")—and my naughtness or complete disappearance as an object of history.

In one of his short stories, Melville wrote: "Think of being a heap of charred offal, like a haltered horse burned in his stall; and all in one flash!" I despair somewhat when I think of this idea of psychological incineration, but what keeps me from deep despair is mainly a common-sense guideline for life: that I can (ought, must, try to, choose to) resonate as gracefully as possible to the great rules and limits of the human biological condition, being aware of my own finiteness; knowing that my days are limited (but not "numbered" in some preordained way); bowing not to indignity or superstition, but to the palpable inevitables, all the while keeping in mind—in the fascinating-to-me juggling act that makes up my life—the responsibilities that I feel in relation to special people in my life, whom I wish, as far as is humanly possible *by me,* to protect from unnecessary pain.

The drama of my own death, when I think about it, intrigues me. It is a fantasy drama that I sometimes rehearse, playing it now one way and then another. My fervent hope is that in the real performance of it, I won't act too badly. The fact is that by and large I do not think about my dying that often—what occupies my mind is living acts, living deeds—but when I do, I deeply desire that the "reviews" of my dying (which, like my death certificate, I shall never be able to see) won't speak too harshly of my way of having done it. It's a point of pride with me.

If I have a recurring model of dying, it is a childish one: sudden and purposeful, sacrificing my life to save a father figure. But I am betrayed by my own unconscious. My actual fantasies of dying have a contradictory quality to them: I fantasize that I die heroically and futilely, dramatically and pointlessly—a near-miss, as perhaps much of my life has been.

I have every reason to believe that I shall see this book in print. However, not inconsistently, I harbor many deep hopes that someday—in the finite future—it will be read posthumously. And then my own cycle of life will have been completed. The thought of that round aspect of life's course makes my having written this book a source of deep satisfaction for me. Those aspects of life—spouse and children, together with beloved teachers, friends and relatives, and my own efforts with patients and students: love and work—are what my life, as one who has been a lucky mortal, is largely about. I weep for everyone in the world's whole history who, either out of unbearable anguish or from enforced misery or pain, has had to write a personal document of death, but I am slightly assuaged by the thought that there exist letters, notes, diaries, utterances and even books that can serve as rutters for someone who is lost on the way to dying and is looking for direction.

Notes

Chapter 1: The Rutters of Death

1. *From The First Voyage Round the World by MAGELLAN,* Translated *from the Accounts of Pigafetta, and other contemporary writers, Accompanied by Original Documents, with notes and an Introduction by Lord Stanley of Alderley* (London: Printed for the Hakluyt Society, 1874).
2. Gordon Allport, *The Use of Personal Documents as Psychological Science* (New York: Social Science Research Council, 1942). A book of letters edited by Allport himself—*Letters from Jenny* (New York: Harcourt, Brace & World, 1965)—is an especially lucid and sympathetic psychological study of one extended set of personal documents: letters of a woman to her son.
3. In *The New York Times Book Review,* June 27, 1976.
4. This book does not contain any documents relating to *subintentioned* deaths or indirect or participative subsuicides. Those are the "natural" or "accidental" or "homicidal" deaths in which the decedent has played some partial, covert, latent—*unconscious*—role in *hastening* his or her own demise. Examples can be found in misuse or neglect of necessary medical treatment (as in diabetes, kidney disease, heart problems, cirrhosis, even cancer), in risk-taking behaviors, abuse of drugs or alcohol, provoking an attack by another, etc. I have written about subintentioned death in *Deaths of Man* (New York: Penguin Books, 1974).

Chapter 3: Self-Destruction

1. Paul Friedman, ed., *On Suicide* (New York: International Universities Press, 1967).
2. Paul Friedman, "Suicide Among Police: A Study of 93 Suicides Among New York City Policemen, 1934–1940," in Edwin S. Shneid-

man, ed., *Essays in Self-Destruction* (New York: Science House, 1967); and Michael F. Heiman, "Police Suicides Revisited," *Suicide*, Spring 1975, Vol. 5, No. 1, pp. 5–20.

3. Yvonne Kapp, *Eleanor Marx* (New York: Pantheon, 1977).
4. From Arthur Koestler, *The Case of the Midwife Toad* (New York: Random House, 1972).
5. From Quentin Bell, *Virginia Woolf—A Biography* (London: Hogarth Press, 1972; New York: Harcourt, Brace, Jovanovich, 1972).
6. From Walter Edwin Peck, *Shelley: His Life and Work*, Vol. I, p. 493 (Boston: Houghton, Mifflin Co., 1927; London: Chatto and Windus, Ltd.).
7. A fascinating account of Elton Hammond's life, together with a series of his letters and his suicide note, appear in *The Diary, Reminiscences and Correspondence of Henry Crabb Robinson*, Vol. III, Chap. 5 (London: Macmillan and Co., 1869).
8. Edwin S. Shneidman, "Suicide Notes Reconsidered," *Psychiatry*, November 1973, Vol. 36, No. 11, pp. 379–394.
9. Margarethe von Andics, *Suicide and the Meaning of Life* (London: William Hodge & Co., 1947).
10. Erwin Ringel, "The Presuicidal Syndrome," *Suicide and Life-Threatening Behavior*, Fall 1976, Vol. 6, No. 3, pp. 131–149.
11. From A. Alvarez, *The Savage God: A Study of Suicide* (New York: Random House, 1972).
12. From Boris Pasternak, *I Remember: Sketch for an Autobiography* (New York: Pantheon, 1959).
13. Selections from *The Dwarf* by Pär Lagerkvist, translated from the Swedish by Alexandra Dick. Copyright © 1945 by L. B. Fisher Publishing Corp. Renewed Copyright © 1973 by L. B. Fisher Publishing Corp. (now a division of Farrar, Straus & Giroux, Inc.).

Chapter 4: Execution

1. In Norman Ault, ed., *Elizabethan Lyrics* (New York: Capricorn Books, 1949), pp. 120–121.
2. Gil Elliot, *The Twentieth Century Book of the Dead* (New York: Charles Scribner's Sons, 1972).

3. Jadwiga Bezwinska, ed., *Amidst a Nightmare of Crime* (Publications of the Panstwowe Muzeum w Oswiecimiu, 1973).
4. From Karl Brocher, ed., *Last Letters from Stalingrad (Letze Briefe aus Stalingrad),* trans. Franz Schneider and Charles Gullans (Copyright © 1961 by The Hudson Review, Inc.).
5. From Helmut Gollwitzer, Kathe Kuhn and Reinhold Schneider, eds., *Dying We Live,* trans. Reinard C. Kuhn (New York: Pantheon, 1956), pp. 173–175.
6. From *Dying We Live,* p. 182.
7. From *Dying We Live,* pp. 133–134.
8. From *Dying We Live,* pp. 279–282.
9. There are several lugubrious books, reflecting millions of murders, filled with letters of Nazi victims. These include: *Dying We Live* and *Amidst a Nightmare of Crime,* cited above; *The Last Hours,* cited below; *I Never Saw Another Butterfly: Children's Drawings and Poems from Terezin Concentration Camp* (New York: McGraw-Hill, n.d.); and Terrence Des Pres, *The Survivor* (New York: Pocket Books, 1977). Des Pres's book contains a comprehensive bibliography of survivors of the concentration camps.
10. *The Last Hours: Farewell Letters of Danish Patriots (De Sidste Timer: Afskedsbreve fra danske Patrioter)* (Copenhagen: Berlingske Forlag, 1945).
11. From Vibeke Malthe-Bruun, *Heroic Heart—The Diary of Kim Malthe-Bruun* (New York: Random House, 1955).
12. From M. Lincoln Schuster, ed., *A Treasury of the World's Great Letters* (New York: Simon and Schuster, 1960), pp. 334–338.
13. Within the same month as John Brown's execution, no less a talent than Herman Melville wrote a haunting poem—one of the best poems ever written by an American—about the event and its veiled implications for the nation. Melville's stark poem conjures up a frightening picture of a weird Christ-like John Brown, his body swaying at the end of the rope, his anguished face covered by the hangman's black hood, all masked except for the defiant beard, which is seen streaming out beneath the hood, ominous in its symbolic meaning. Prophetically, as though he were reading the future, Melville entitled his poem "The Portent."

Hanging from the beam,
Slowly swaying (such the law),
Gaunt the shadow on your green.
Shenandoah!
The cut is on the crown
(Lo, John Brown),
And the stabs shall heal no more.

Hidden in the cap
Is the anguish none can draw;
So the future veils its face,
Shenandoah!
But the streaming beard is shown
(Weird John Brown),
The meteor of the war.

14. *A Treasury of the World's Great Letters,* pp. 497–499.
15. Frederick F. Wagner, "Suicide Notes," *Danish Medical Journal,* 1960, Vol. 7, pp. 62–64.
16. Eugene Loebl was born in Slovakia in 1907. He became a leading Marxist theoretician in Czechoslovakia. As head of the Ministry of Foreign Trade, he came into conflict with the Soviet Union, and was sentenced to life imprisonment in the Slansky trials of 1952. Released after eleven years, he was appointed director of the State Bank in 1963. When the Russians invaded in 1968, he fled to the West. He then became professor of economics and political science at Vassar College, where he remained until his retirement in 1976. His books include *Mental Work; The Real Source of Wealth; Stalinism in Prague; The Intellectual Revolution: Marxism, Boon or Dead End; Economy at the Crossroads; Humanomics; My Mind on Trial* (1977); *The Responsible Society,* with Stephen Roman (1978). Mr. Loebl is a member of the board of advisers of the Slovak World Congress. He lives in New York City.
17. *A Treasury of the World's Great Letters,* pp. 299–304.

Chapter 5: Malignancy

1. A. Draper, C. W. Dupertuis and J. L. Caughley, *Human Constitution in Clinical Medicine* (New York: Hoeber, 1944).
2. Elisabeth Kübler-Ross, *On Death and Dying* (New York: Macmillan, 1969).
3. Loma Feigenberg, *Terminalvård: En metod för psykologisk vård av döende cancerpatienter* (Lund: LiberLaromedel, 1977). (To be published in English under the title *Terminal Care: Terminal Friendship Contracts* by Brunner/Mazel in New York.)
4. Henry A. Murray, *Explorations in Personality* (London and New York: Oxford University Press, 1938).
5. John Hinton, "The Influences of Previous Personality on Reactions to Having Terminal Cancer," *Omega*, 1975, Vol. 6, No. 2, pp. 95–111.
6. Susan Sontag, *Illness as Metaphor* (New York: Farrar, Straus & Giroux, 1978).
7. Edwin S. Shneidman, "Some Aspects of Psychotherapy with Dying Persons," in Charles A. Garfield, ed., *Psychosocial Care of the Dying Patient* (New York: McGraw-Hill, 1978).
8. Cicely Saunders, "St. Christopher's Hospice," in E. S. Shneidman, ed., *Death: Current Perspectives* (Palo Alto, Cal.: Mayfield Publishing Co., 1976), pp. 516–522.
9. Archie Hanlan, "Notes of a Dying Professor" and "More Notes of a Dying Professor," *Pennsylvania Gazette,* March 1972, Vol. 70, No. 3, pp. 18–24; and February 1973, Vol. 71, No. 4, pp. 29–32. Reprinted with permission of Mrs. Mary S. Hanlan. Also published as part of Archie J. Hanlan, *Autobiography of Dying* (New York: Doubleday & Co., 1978).
10. From Vilhelm Moberg, *The Emigrants (Utvandrara)* (1951; New York: Popular Library, 1978).
11. From Hans Zinsser, *As I Remember Him* (Boston: Little, Brown, 1940), pp. 439–440.
12. From Stewart Alsop, *Stay of Execution,* pp. 9–11. Copyright © 1973 by J. B. Lippincott Co.

13. Eugene Trombley, "A Psychiatrist's Response to a Life-Threatening Illness," *Life-Threatening Behavior,* 1972, Vol. 2, No. 1, pp. 26–34.
14. Hubert H. Humphrey, *The Education of a Public Man* (Garden City, N.Y.: Doubleday and Co., 1976).
15. *Reader's Digest,* August 1977.
16. *The New York Times,* October 26, 1977. Copyright © by The New York Times Company.
17. *Minneapolis Tribune,* December 23, 1977.

Chapter 7: Mourning

1. Edwin S. Shneidman, *Deaths of Man* (New York: Penguin Books, 1974), pp. 33–42.
2. Erich Lindemann et al., "Preventive Intervention in a Four-Year-Old Child Whose Father Committed Suicide," in Albert C. Cain, ed., *Survivors of Suicide* (Springfield, Ill.: C. C. Thomas, 1972).
3. Colin Murray Parkes, *Bereavement* (New York: International Universities Press, 1972).
4. Erich Lindemann, "Symptomatology and Management of Acute Grief," *American Journal of Psychiatry,* 1944, Vol. 101, pp. 141–148.
5. Chad Varah, *The Samaritans* (New York: Macmillan, 1966).
6. Martha Wolfenstein, *Disaster: A Psychological Essay* (New York: Macmillan, 1957).
7. Paul Friedman and L. Lum, "Some Psychiatric Notes on the *Andrea Doria* Disaster," *American Journal of Psychiatry,* 1957, Vol. 114, pp. 426–432.
8. A. Wallace, *Tornado in Worcester* (Washington, D.C.: National Research Council, 1956).
9. From Robert Jay Lifton, *Death in Life: Survivors of Hiroshima* (New York: Random House, 1967).

Chapter 8: Toward a Better Death

1. Avery D. Weisman, *On Dying and Denying* (New York: Behavioral Publications, 1972).
2. Lyn Helton, "Soon There Will Be No More Me," *West* magazine, *Los Angeles Times,* January 16, 1972, pp. 8–13. Copyright © 1971. Reprinted with permission of the Jennifer Elizabeth Helton Trust, Denver, Colorado.
3. From Victor Richards, *Cancer: The Wayward Cell.* Copyright © 1972 by the Regents of the University of California.
4. From John Hinton, *Dying* (Baltimore: Penguin Books, 1967); with permission.
5. Jory Graham, "A Time to Live . . ." *Chicago Daily News,* July 9, 1977.
6. Henry A. Murray, "Dead to the World: The Passions of Herman Melville," in E. S. Shneidman, ed., *Essays in Self-Destruction* (New York: Science House, 1967), pp. 7–29. Dr. Murray reminded me that first credit for this phrase belongs to Otto Rank, who, in his book *Art and the Artist* (New York: Alfred A. Knopf, 1932, p. 64)—discussing the theoretical differences between the artist and the neurotic—speaks of the "volitional affirmation of the obligatory"—even, in the case of the artist, of the Oedipus conflict.
7. Baldassare Castiglione, *The Book of the Courtier,* trans. Charles S. Singleton (Garden City, N.Y.: Anchor Books, 1959; originally published in 1528).
8. Letter from Pastor Paul Schneider to his wife, November 7, 1937. In Helmut Gollwitzer et al., eds., *Dying We Live* (New York: Pantheon Books, 1956), pp. 14–15.
9. From Stephen C. Pepper, "Can a Philosophy Make One Philosophical?" in E. S. Shneidman, ed., *Essays in Self-Destruction* (New York: Science House [now Jason Aronson], 1967, pp. 114–128).
10. Stephen C. Pepper, *World Hypotheses* (Berkeley and Los Angeles: University of California Press, 1942).

Index

Excerpts from *The New York Times* from the November 7, 1968, July 12, 1972, and October 26, 1977 issues. Copyright © 1968, 1972, and 1977 by The New York Times Company. Reprinted by permission.

Excerpt from "The Influences of Previous Personality on Reactions to Having Terminal Cancer" by John Hinton. Reprinted by permission of *Omega Journal of Death and Dying.*

Excerpt from *I Remember,* by Boris Pasternak, translated by David Magarshack. Copyright 1959 by Pantheon Books. Reprinted by permission of Pantheon Books, a Division of Random House, Inc.

Excerpts from *Moments of Being: Unpublished Autobiographical Writings of Virginia Woolf,* edited by Jeanne Schulkind. Reprinted by permission of Harcourt Brace Jovanovich, Inc.

Excerpt from *The Savage God* by A. Alvarez. Copyright © 1970, 1971, 1972 by A. Alvarez. Reprinted by permission of Random House, Inc.

Excerpt from *The Case of the Midwife Toad,* by Arthur Koestler. Copyright © 1971 by Arthur Koestler. Reprinted by permission of Random House, Inc.

Excerpt from *New York Jew,* by Alfred Kazin. Copyright © 1978 by Alfred Kazin. Reprinted by permission of Random House, Inc.

Excerpt from *Beyond All This Fiddle* by A. Alvarez. Copyright © 1968 by A. Alvarez. Reprinted by permission of Random House, Inc.

Excerpt from "Can a Philosophy Make One Philosophical?" by Stephen C. Pepper. New York: Science House, 1967. Reprinted by permission of Science House.

Excerpt from *World of Wonders* by Robertson Davies. Reprinted by permission of the Macmillan Company of Canada Limited.

Excerpt from *World of Wonders.* Copyright © 1975 by Robertson Davies, published by Viking Press. Reprinted by permission of The Macmillan Company of Canada Limited and Curtis Brown.

Excerpt from *The Letters of Sacco and Vanzetti,* edited by Marion Deman Frankfurter and Gardner Jackson. Copyright © 1928 by The Viking Press, Inc., copyright © renewed 1956 by The Viking Press, Inc. Reprinted by permission of Viking Penguin, Inc.

About the Author

Edwin S. Shneidman, Ph.D., is Professor of Thanatology and Director of the Laboratory for the Study of Life-Threatening Behavior at the University of California at Los Angeles School of Medicine. He was formerly co-director (and co-founder) of the Los Angeles Suicide Prevention Center and was the charter director of the Center for the Study of Suicide Prevention at the National Institute of Mental Health in Bethesda. He has been a Public Health Service Special Research Fellow and Visiting Professor at Harvard and a Fellow at the Center for Advanced Study in the Behavioral Sciences (at Stanford). He has been president of two divisions (Clinical and Public Service) of the American Psychological Association and was founder-president of the American Association of Suicidology. His books include: as editor, *Thematic Test Analysis, Essays in Self-Destruction, On the Nature of Suicide, Death and the College Student, Suicidology: Contemporary Developments* and *Death: Current Perspectives;* as co-editor, *Clues to Suicide, The Cry for Help, Aspects of Depression* and *The Psychology of Suicide;* as author, *Deaths of Man* (nominated for the 1973 National Book Award in Science). He is also the author of over a hundred articles on death and suicide, including ones for the *Encyclopaedia Britannica, Comprehensive Textbook of Psychiatry* and *Psychiatric Annals.* He is married and has four sons, all health professionals.

BD
444
.S48

1980